FROGS
MATTER
M⬤ST

A Parable About Taking the Personal and Professional Leadership Leap

Jack R. Christianson, PhD
and Ron M. Tracy

MILLENNIAL PRESS
& DISTRIBUTION

1699 North 210 East
Orem, UT 84057
www.millennialpress.com

FROGS MATTER MOST
Jack R. Christianson, PhD and Ron M. Tracy

Cover Design: Adam Riggs
Book Design: LibrisPro

ISBN: 978-1-932597-69-1

Printed in the United States of America
1 2 3 4 5 6 7 8 9 10   20 19 18 17 16

Printed in the United States of America

For Max L. Pinegar, William R. Siddoway, and Bob Parrott who have taught us the real value of people and nature and how to lead, inspire and prepare others to take the leadership leap. Thank you for your examples of leadership in your own environments.

Acknowledgments

Every author knows that no book ever comes to fruition without the help of many individuals. With deep appreciation, we thank Deniece Tracy for her idea of using a frog to teach us about leadership, and Melanie Christianson for her constant feedback and support.

We also want to thank Randy and Ryan Bott, a great father and son team at Millennial Press, who guided us through the publishing process; James Parkinson for his kind foreword and continued support of this project; and Bailey Rees for her artistic abilities. A special thanks to Karlene Browning for her patience with us and her superior editing skills; and to Adam Riggs for his cover design.

Last of all, we thank anyone who has the imagination and courage to learn from a frog and realize the value of people.

Table of Contents

Foreword

by James W. Parkinson

Jack Christianson and Ron Tracy are two of the most gifted leaders I have ever met, so I was not surprised they decided to write a book together on the subject. What did surprise me was how effortlessly they used their "story telling" speaking skills to create such an important and readable book as *Frogs Matter Most.*

Over the last five years I have spoken to over 22,000 high school and college students across America. Contrary to popular myth our young people are not a lost generation of self-centered ciphers waiting for an unearned inheritance. They are young men and women waiting to be led and their opportunity to lead. My message to them is simple: you matter. Take personal responsibility for your own education and life. *Frogs Matter Most* is the next logical step.

Frogs Matter Most is not just about leadership. It's a powerful lesson on the meaning of our lives. What is the most important principle on which we should base our lives? Success? Money? Power? Christianson and Tracy answer that question and reveal the genius of putting other people first. Like the masterful story-tellers they are, they make their case through metaphor.

Every person, young or old, new or seasoned, who aspires to make a difference in life should read this book. At age 66, reading *Frogs Matter Most* caused me to stop and make sure I was on the right path. For that reminder alone I am grateful.

James W. Parkinson is a prominent California attorney, speaker and author of *Autodidactic: Self-Taught, Soldier Slaves: Abandoned by the White House, Courts and Congress,* and *The Big Three and Me*, with Billy Casper and Lee Benson.

Introduction

Jack R. Christianson:

In April 1984 I attended a book signing for one of my favorite authors, Og Mandino. I had read nearly every book he had written, and several, multiple times. When we first met, Mr. Mandino, noticing the number of his books in my arms, kindly looked me in the eye and politely said, "You must be a real fan!"

I responded with a star-struck reply about how he had inspired me and that I hoped to be an author like him someday.

"What have you written so far?" he asked.

In complete naivety I told him and then offered him a copy of my first publication, an audio speech. At that moment, Og proved he lived the messages from his books and speeches. He accepted the autographed copy and then gently took hold of both of my hands. He looked squarely into my eyes as though the two of us were the only ones in the store. He promised he would listen to my recording. He sincerely thanked me and genuinely expressed his love. I was inspired! Og became real to me that night.

People mattered most to him. I was inspired to follow such a leader: a leader who possessed that rare quality of understanding that great leaders *always* value people. Since that time, I have searched for leaders to inspire me in such a way that I would choose to follow them. Very early on in that search, I decided to strive to be the kind of leader that I looked for in others. I focused my doctoral studies on researching how to help students and educational institutions be more successful and how to effectively lead a thriving, efficient organization. This parable of a frog and two businessmen is partially the result of my research and experience.

Og Mandino and others have motivated and inspired me to excellence in every level of leadership. Hopefully, *Frogs Matter Most* with its three core values, eight leadership behaviors and the four leadership roles can do the same for you and any organization. Leaders lead, inspire, motivate, and maintain motivation. They give life to their vision and they work to instill that vision in all with whom they associate. They walk the walk and they talk the talk! Great leaders understand that they must lead themselves before they can lead and inspire others. Their life is their message! No one will be perfect at leadership. No one. Yet all leaders can be perfect at trying and always striving to be a little better each day at *what they do, how they do it, and knowing why they do it!*

Ron M. Tracy:

Perhaps now, more than ever, organizations, governments, and individuals are desperate for true leadership. Inspirational leaders are few and far between. We hope to close that gap by introducing you to the Values of the Pond and the Leadership Behaviors and Roles. This book will teach you the correct leadership roles and behaviors to use in any situation to confidently achieve a positive outcome—every time.

I searched for years to find a book, manual, or training course that taught a step-by-step process anyone could follow to become a leader. I never found one that could take any person from where they are now to assuming a successful leadership role. Leadership can indeed be taught, so these concepts were developed.

You can be an inspiring leader. You can learn how to be the kind of leader you want to be. All you have to do is embrace the principles that Bob (who happens to be a frog) teaches—behave like a leader and make your own pond the best it can be!

We had a wonderful time writing *Frogs Matter Most*, and I hope you have just as much fun reading it. Always… No, never… No, always remember—Frogs and People Do Matter Most.

Frogs Matter Most

*B*rad paced back and forth, wringing his hands with deep anxiety. It felt like every part of his body wanted to go in different directions at the same time. Beads of sweat gathered on his upper lip as the agonizing thought kept repeating in his mind. *How did I let Mike get me into this predicament?* Mike, his boss and close friend, had been promoted last week and just yesterday had offered Brad the opportunity to be his replacement. As he looked at the walnut paneled office with the oversized desk, full bookshelves, and the stuffed leather chair that came with the new assignment, Brad asked himself out loud, "I thought we were friends. Did he think he was doing me a favor?"

Anxiety continued sweeping over Brad as he worried. *Have I bitten off too much, too soon in my career to accept such a responsible position?* Mike, several years his senior, had expressed genuine confidence and trust in Brad's abilities while offering the opportunity. There was no way he wanted to let Mike down by giving in to his own fears and insecurity.

As he continued pondering upon his situation, the anxiety increased. *How will I ever measure up to Mike? He is by far the best leader I've ever worked for.* When Mike came into the same position several years earlier, he had taken over the worst division in the company. Within a few months the division became one of the most productive. He was a true leader. Just about everybody who worked with him improved their skills and individual performance. His people enjoyed coming to work and working together as a team. Mike inspired complete loyalty to him and his vision. His people would follow him anywhere. How can you compete with a natural born leader?

The anxiety was getting the best of Brad. He didn't think he could do it. He didn't know how to do it. He didn't know what to do. Just as he was picking up the phone to call Mike and let him know he had changed his mind, Mike walked through the door.

"You look just like me when I first took this job," observed Mike. "I sat in that same chair thinking I had made the biggest mistake of my life!"

Brad answered with exasperation and palms motioning upward, "What have you done to me? I can't see the troops rallying behind me like they've done for you. I don't even know where to begin."

"That's exactly what I wanted to hear!" exclaimed Mike.

"You've got to be kidding," replied Brad. "I just admitted I don't have a clue how I'm going to do this job and you seem happy about it!"

"When you can admit you don't have a clue, that's when you know you're ready to start the process of becoming an impactful leader. Let's get one thing clear right now. A leader who thinks he or she has all the answers all the time, is only a manager, not a leader.

Mike walked over to Brad and put his hand on Brad's shoulder. "Your statement confirms I chose the right guy. This division doesn't need another person who thinks they already know it all. It needs a leader who is humble enough to realize its people are the most important element and that their input, creativity and innovation are the keys to success. In other words, frogs matter most!"

Brad looked up at Mike, stunned and a little confused. "What are you talking about?" he interjected. "Don't you mean people matter most?"

"Nope, I mean frogs matter most."

"What's going on here? Have you got a hangover or something? I don't get it. What am I missing? I thought your mantra was, 'People matter most.' What do frogs have to do with people?"

Mike couldn't help but laugh out loud. Pointing out the window he said, "You see that parking lot outside? Remember when it used to be a big pond?"

"Of course," said Brad. "We all used to love strolling around the pond, watching the fish jump and the ducks and geese fly in and out. The frogs would make that funny croaking sound and hop from the lily pads into the water when we walked too close. I kind of miss the pond. It was a great place to clear your head and think."

"That's right. And that's what I meant by, frogs matter most. When I first took this job, I sat in this office for days, not leaving, afraid I would make mistakes with my people. What if I said the wrong thing? What if they didn't like me? What if they didn't accept me as their boss? How would I get them to do their jobs? How would we meet quotas as a division? How could we get better each day? And, what kind of leader was I going to be? How would they compare me to their previous bosses? I had all kinds of questions, doubts and fears.

"Then, the situation got worse! In the middle of all this turmoil my good friend and mentor passed away. He had taught and inspired me more than anyone on what it meant to be a leader. In fact, he made such a huge impact on me that when I got home from his funeral I sat down and wrote my thoughts and feelings about this incredible, influential leader. Every Monday morning

I pull the paper out of my desk drawer and reread the things I wrote. It's a constant reminder to keep trying to be the kind of leader he inspired me to be. I've never shared what I wrote with anyone, but given your obvious anxiety about your new position, I feel the time is right. This is sacred stuff to me so please treat it with respect."

"You know I will," said Brad. "Thanks for trusting me enough to share something so personal. I'll treat this with the respect it deserves."

"Thanks," said Mike. "I know you will, or I wouldn't be sharing it with you now. I wanted to capture the thoughts and feelings I had for my mentor before the memories began to fade. I kept the paper but also transferred them into my daily journal."

Mike reached into his coat pocket and pulled out a wrinkled and dog-eared piece of yellow notepad paper. He carefully unfolded it and began to read.

> The sun was warm on my skin as I followed the pallbearers and the casket. It seemed unusually warm for late February. Perhaps it was what I felt inside that warmed me. The man whose body lay in the casket had been my mentor, teacher, friend, and leader. I had known him since I was a kid and had tried to be like him and to learn from him.
>
> Of course, he wasn't perfect but he understood the human experience and he was real. His feet had been firmly grounded in humility and confidence. He knew who he was and what he stood for. He was mindful of his gifts and talents yet, was not full of himself. Nor did he see himself as one who was better than others because he had

experienced great success throughout his life of eighty-two years.

Although he had held many positions of influence and had led companies with thousands of people, he was approachable, and I always felt comfortable in his presence. He never hesitated to correct me or chastise me, if necessary. But, he did so in such a way that motivated me to be better. I never felt inferior or less important because I had made mistakes. He led me and now he is gone.

All my life I have sought to find leaders who would lead me. I have looked for men and women, leaders, who would show me the way to success and teach me how to do what they had done. I have always wanted to be led by those who truly inspired and motivated me to action, but I did not want to be pushed, commanded, coerced, manipulated, or guilt-tripped into doing things they desired of me.

This man possessed all of the qualities and attributes I'd been looking for. What he carried with him was more than skill, more than strategies, more than theories; he was a leader. He led himself and therefore could, without hypocrisy or intimidation, lead others. Again, he was not perfect and he made mistakes, but he so inspired me that I wanted to follow him and be led by him.

Now, as I walked behind the casket and watched

the six pallbearers place it into the back of the hearse, I was filled with warmth and joy to think that I'd had a lifetime of being led by such a leader. He understood and lived the principle, "Effective teaching is the very essence of leadership." He understood that people reach their full potential, both professionally and personally, through change and discipline in their lives. They cannot be coerced. They must be led, and that means teaching!

We are all teachers! Therefore, we are all leaders! We are all learners. As we each make our way through our lives we must learn to learn, teach, and lead. I have tried to pattern my leadership style according to what I have looked for in those I have wanted to lead me. I have sought to incorporate in my leadership what I desired in a leader.

Brad was obviously touched. "I had no idea that you'd been so influenced by your mentor. Who was he?"

"His name was Max. He was my uncle, but I also had many opportunities to see him as a leader in the business community, to associate with and be led by him. We had many late night discussions where he taught me, as well as corrected me on many of the mistakes he had observed me make."

Mike chuckled. "Don't get me wrong. It was never comfortable, but it was always beneficial. I felt his support and concern for my success, and I knew everything he did was for my benefit. I began to find my way as a leader because Max saw the potential for what I could become instead of what I appeared to be at the time."

"Sounds like a great guy," said Brad.

"He was. And he was very much to me what Morrie Schwartz was to Mitch Albon in Mitch's book, *Tuesdays with Morrie*." Mike walked over to the bookshelf and looked over his collection until he found a book that looked like it had been read several times. There were bookmarks in many places but he knew the one he wanted. After opening the book to the right page he continued.

"Albon wrote of his professor, Morrie Schwartz. 'Have you ever really had a teacher (leader)? One who saw you as a raw but precious thing, a jewel that, with wisdom, could be polished to a proud shine? If you are lucky enough to find your way to such teachers (leaders), you will always find your way back.'"

Mike looked up at Brad. "I added the word 'leader' next to the word 'teacher' for a reason. Because I believe as Max believed, that teaching is the very essence of leadership. If we teach, we lead. If we lead, we teach."

Mike walked back to the bookshelf and pulled another volume from the top shelf. He opened the book to a well-marked place and said. "John Wooden, the legendary coach of the UCLA Bruin's basketball team said it this way: 'In the eyes of most observers, my title is 'Coach Wooden,' but this is not what I would list first on my resume or business card. From my earliest years I have viewed my primary job as one of educating others: I am a teacher. I believe effective leaders are first and foremost, good teachers. We are in the education business. Whether in the classroom or on the court, my job was the same: to effectively teach those under my super-vision how to perform to the best of their ability in ways that best served the goals of our team. I believe the same is true for produc-tive leaders in any organization."

Mike looked up and nodded at Brad. Then found another highlighted place in the book and continued reading. " 'What is your title? Call yourself a teacher. Put it on your business card and remember it well. However, I will confess that just calling yourself a teacher is not enough. You must also know how to teach."'

Mike closed the book and put it on the desk. "This is the bedrock of my approach to leadership. Max gave me a solid foundation and the motivation to be a leader, but I never realized how little I knew until I met Bob."

"Bob?" asked Brad.

"I'm getting to him. The day after Max's funeral I realized I was alone for the first time. Max, my mentor and teacher, was gone and everything now rested squarely on my shoulders. I was every bit as overwhelmed as you are right now. I was a nervous wreck. I paced, sat, fidgeted, worried, and kept looking out the window of this office. I finally came to the point where I knew I couldn't sit in my office all day. I had to do something. I had to act. I pondered again and again on what Max had taught me. He wouldn't have tolerated my inaction, but I still didn't know what actions I needed to take. As I was mentally trying to formulate a plan of action, my eyes kept turning to the pond outside our office building. That pond no longer exists. As you know, it has become a sterile parking lot. But when it did exist it provided a better classroom than my MBA at the university."

"So, what'd you see?" asked Brad with a questioning look.

"Well, I keep this part closer to my vest than even the journal entry about Max. I figure people would think I was completely off my rocker."

"You're sounding more and more mysterious," Brad said.

"Let me see if I can help you understand. Max taught me the value of being a true leader and teacher. My second mentor, who lived in the pond, taught me how to incorporate Max's teachings and so much more. I'm deeply saddened that wonderful leadership training ground has been replaced by an uninspiring parking lot."

"I'm not sure I'm following you, but you have my attention," Brad replied. "Help me understand something first. I always thought people were natural leaders. You're either born a leader or you aren't. Are you telling me you can learn to be a leader?"

"Leadership is like any other skill set. It might be harder to learn how to be a leader, but it can certainly be taught, practiced and, sometimes perfected. Brad, I believe you're the right guy for this job because you have the ability to learn how to become a leader. And I'm willing to put the time and effort into teaching you the same things I've learned. So, I'm going to tell you all about what I learned while watching the frogs in the pond."

Brad responded, "I don't mean to sound skeptical, but this thing is getting weirder by the minute. Frogs in the pond! Don't tell me the frogs spoke to you and imparted all their frog wisdom and leadership secrets."

"Well, that's exactly what I'm going to tell you. However, I only talked to one frog. Now, before you call and have me committed, I want you to think about all the Disney characters. Almost every character is a talking animal of some sort. Whether it's a mouse, a duck, a chipmunk or even Mr. Toad, they all talk. The kids all listen to them, and they love it. To children, it's simple. The animals are as real as any human they know. At times, they're even more credible than the adults in their lives. I don't think you would say Walt Disney was a failure or needed to be committed. His desire was that you use your imagination to see the real world around you in a different way. In addition, do you recall that C.S. Lewis used talking animals to teach important principles? All I'm asking you, Brad, is to use your imagination. Don't be so sophisticated that you can't learn something from the natural world around us."

"I've always looked up to you, Mike, and I know what you do works. But, you've got me teetering. I'll keep my phone in my pocket for a while longer and see where this leads."

"Fair enough. Just hang in there with me. My hope is you'll learn the things that will assist you to become the leader you desire to be."

"Okay," Brad said hesitatingly. "It sounds pretty weird. This could be a real hard sell, Mike. You've got your work cut out for you if you expect me to believe a frog actually talked to you. But, I'll listen. If you believe it'll help me become the kind of leader you are, I'll give you an ear."

"I don't want you to become the kind of leader I am. You need to become the kind of leader you were meant to be. You have unique talents and skills. Learn to use them in a way that works best for you, not for me or for anyone else. I can help you do that."

Frogs Matter Most

- *It's okay to ask for help*

- *People matter most*

- *Leadership is teaching*

- *Leadership can be learned*

2

Taking the Leap

*M*ike stopped and sighed with relief. "Brad, I haven't told this story to anyone because it sounds so unbelievable. Are you still with me or do you think I've gone off the edge?"

"I'm reserving my judgment," Brad replied. "But if all this helped you become the leader you are, and it'll help me become the leader I want to be, I'll go off the edge with you!"

"Before we go any further, I want to tell you one of the most important things I learned from this entire experience. You have to choose what kind of leader you want to be. You must decide where you will focus your attention. Many people at this starting point decide that profitability and getting the work done is their main concern. The people who do the work come second."

"I get that," said Brad. "I've had a few bosses like that."

"Me, too," said Mike. "To them, bottom-line dollars are the most important thing. We call these people managers. Others decide that people are the most important consideration. Taking care of their people is the most important thing and bottom line is secondary. We call these people mentors."

"That's a good distinction," said Brad. "Managers versus

mentors. There really is a difference between the two. But where do leaders come in?"

"Great question," said Mike. "Leaders must choose both. They get things done and they value people. A leader combines the best of managing and mentoring. There are no shortcuts or easy outs. That's why very few people achieve the role of leader. If you can't develop both skills, you should, at the very least, have the humility to hire people who have expertise in the areas that aren't your strong points."

"Sounds good to me," responded Brad. "And I think I've made my choice. I don't want my career to be mediocre. I'm not sure how to be both a manager and a mentor, but I'm willing to learn. I'm ready to get going!"

"I hoped that's what you'd say, Brad. That's why I chose you in the first place. Now that you've made your decision, let's get on with the story."

I was a nervous wreck when I took this new job. I had all kinds of doubts and questions about leading my division. The first few weeks were awful! The meetings were endless. My managers expected me to perform miracles. My direct reports were testing the boundaries to see how I would respond to a multitude of performance problems and other issues. It felt like I was in the middle of the ocean in a tiny boat. I'd never felt so alone in my life.

One day while I was sitting at my desk looking out the office window at the pond, I noticed something peculiar. As I looked closer, it seemed that the pond was divided into sections. It also appeared that there was a frog in charge of each section. These lead frogs sat on their lily pads and oversaw the other frogs.

At first I thought I was seeing things, but the longer I watched, the more I saw. I even opened the side window to see if I could hear anything that would be helpful.

There was one particular lead frog that stood out. He was different from all the others. Most of the other lead frogs made all kinds of noises and gestures at the other frogs. I know it sounds crazy, but from where I sat, it looked as though they were shouting at the other frogs. Sometimes they would hop over to another frog, get right in their face, and command the frog to do something. Their methods seemed to be quite intimidating.

The lead frog that stood out never did those things. He was every bit in control as the other lead frogs, but he didn't need force and yelling to get things done. It looked like he had created a real team of frogs. Not only that, but his section was cleaner and more organized.

He was the one I decided to watch the closest because his style appeared to be so peculiar. In fact, he reminded me of John Wooden in his book, *Wooden on Leadership*. Wooden realized that when he yelled at the players he only made himself look foolish and the players mad. After his first few years of coaching, he made a promise to himself never to get mad or yell at his players again. It made all the difference in his coaching career.

At first, I noticed my frog engaging in different ways with each of his frogs. It seemed as though they were actually having conversations of some sort. The thing that intrigued me most was he wasn't yelling or screaming. He would say something and then give the other frog equal time to communicate.

I couldn't believe what I was seeing and hearing. Maybe it was all in my mind. Perhaps I was grasping at anything that would help me in my own situation. But one thing was certain, this lead frog got better results from his frogs than the other lead frogs. I also noticed that his frogs seemed happier than the other frogs in the pond. They were working as a real team. Something was going on and I had to find out what it was—and quick!

I jumped right out of my chair, ran down the stairs, and out the front door of the building. I made my way to the edge of the pond, hoping to observe this incredible demonstration of leadership from a closer vantage point. In my enthusiasm I made no effort to approach them quietly. The minute I got too close they sounded the alarm and each frog immediately leaped into the water and hid under the lily pads.

I watched for several minutes but all I saw were little green noses just above the surface, waiting for me to go away. I backed up slowly, watching what would occur when I was no longer invading their apparent "business operations." Once I got to a certain point from the pond, they tentatively began to return to their lily pads and their work.

I approached again, more slowly this time. As I moved forward I began talking softly to the lead frog, "I'm not here to hurt you. I am here to learn from you. I've been watching you. The relationship you have with your frogs is so different from the other lead frogs and your results are so much better. I have to know what you're doing."

I moved closer to the pond, walking very slowly and reassuring the frog with each step. When I got to the edge, he was still on his pad staring at me, but ready to leap in an instant. I started to sit down but the movement alarmed him. He croaked loudly and all the frogs leaped back into the water to the security and cover of the lily pads.

There was no going back now. I waited for the frogs to return to the top of the lily pads and the shoreline. It took a good ten minutes before my frog cautiously climbed back on his pad and sat in front of me once more. We looked at each other. Neither of us moved.

I checked my watch and realized I'd spent forty-five minutes to get to this point and I had to get back to the office. I couldn't sit and stare at the frog all day. I needed to get back to my responsibilities.

Slowly I stood up, hoping not to frighten the lead frog. As hard as
I tried to be non-threatening, my movement scared all the frogs
back into the water, except my frog. As our eyes stayed focused
on each other, I saw an almost imperceptible nod from him. Was
I gaining his trust? I'd have to wait to see what tomorrow would
bring. I turned around and went back to my office.

I have to admit I didn't get a thing done the rest of the day. I
spent the time trying to figure out how I was going to communicate with this frog. Some kind of frog treat sounded like the best
bet, so I went to the pet store and bought a package of frog food.

The next day I was down at the pond as soon as I could break
away. I approached even more slowly this time and it worked!
Soon, I was three feet away from my frog, offering him food in the
palm of my hand. He stared at the food, then he stared at me and
turned his back. It was obvious he wasn't interested in the food.

The next day I tried the same thing with a couple of dead flies
I'd picked up on the windowsill that morning. The good thing is
he didn't turn his back to me again but he still wouldn't take the
flies. For the rest of the week I was at the pond, offering any kind
of frog food I could think of with no results. I went back each time
to my office pretty frustrated that I hadn't made any headway.

Over the weekend I pondered what I could do to gain his
trust. I decided to forget the food and just talk to him again.

Early Monday morning I approached the pond with out-
stretched hands and began talking to him. Honestly, I felt pretty
ridiculous, talking to a frog at the edge of a pond. I told him I
didn't want to hurt him or any of the frogs in the pond. I talked
about my new promotion and how unsure I was about leading
a division. Pretty soon, the words just came tumbling out of my
mouth. I opened up about my worries, concerns, and the problems I was currently dealing with and my apprehension about
taking the wrong kinds of actions with my people. In a way, it was
therapeutic just to vocalize my worries.

The frog sat still and stared at me the entire time. But it wasn't the kind of blank stare you usually get from an animal or reptile. He seemed to understand everything I was saying. I swear I could see genuine concern on his face.

And then it happened. Without any kind of warning he spoke. "What can I do for you?" he asked.

I couldn't believe my ears. I thought I was hallucinating! No way was this real! Frogs can't talk! I was entirely speechless. He gazed at me with an incredulous look on his face and asked again, "Is there anything I can do for you?"

He looked as astonished as I was!

I finally came to my senses enough to sputter, "You're talking in my language!"

He retorted, "No, you're talking in mine!"

We both sat in silence, musing over this extraordinary development. Finally, I got control of myself and remembered why I had come to the edge of the pond. Without hesitation I said, "I've been watching you for quite a while and have noticed a few things. Do you mind if I ask you some questions?"

He had overcome his shock as well and answered, "Not at all. I wish you would. I'd like to know what's going on as much as you."

"Okay, here goes. You may think I'm crazy but it looks to me like there are several sections in the pond and there is a lead frog over each section. You are one of the lead frogs, aren't you?"

"Yes, there are, and yes, I am. All the lead frogs sit on a lily pad and oversee the work of each section," he replied.

With a deep breath I continued. "I've also noticed you have a different style from all the other lead frogs. It looks like you discuss things with your frogs. The other lead frogs make loud noises, point, and it appears they coerce their workers. Your relationship seems to be more friendly and inclusive. Have I got that right? If so, I'd like to know what you are doing and why you're doing it."

The frog thought for a moment and said, "I can see some peculiar forces at work here and for some reason we understand each other. Not only that, I seem to suddenly understand everything about your world. I know all about cars, planes, businesses, different countries, and billions of people. This world is certainly much bigger than we frogs ever thought. And look at all of the things you humans have built and accomplished! It's amazing! Is it the same for you?"

"Yes!" I said. "As weird as it sounds, it's like I've been living in the pond, right beside you. I have a deeper understanding of frogs and their lives than I could have ever thought possible!"

Bob nodded in agreement. We sat in silence for a minute until he spoke. "Since you have come to me, it looks like I'm supposed to be your teacher, and you, my student. And since we completely understand each other's worlds, we won't waste time trying to decipher what each word or name means. Does that make sense to you?"

"That's how I see it too," I exclaimed loud enough to startle some of the frogs that were watching. They immediately sounded the alarm and jumped into the water, but not my frog. He sat still and waited for me to finish. "I'd give just about anything to learn how you have become, what looks like to me, such an effective leader."

"Thank you," he said. "Let me introduce myself. I am known in the pond as Bob. We like to watch you humans walk around the pond. It's quite comical to us. Some time ago I was watching a young boy throwing rocks into the pond. Suddenly he threw a rock at me and called me Bob. He continued to throw rocks at me, calling me Bob each time. The other frogs heard it and, as a joke, quit calling me by my given name and started calling me Bob. It stuck. What started as a joke has now become my identity. Everyone knows me as Bob."

"Glad to meet you, Bob," I said. "My name is Mike."

Taking the Leap

- *Choose to take the leadership leap*

- *Choose to have passion*

- *Leaders inspire—not manipulate*

3

Building Trust

*O*h, come on!" blurted Brad. "You've got to be kidding me! You don't expect me to believe this one, do you?"

Mike smiled and patiently said, "I don't care if you believe me or not. I didn't ask you to believe me. I asked you to listen and commit to do whatever it takes to be the kind of leader you want to become. Do you want to be the type of leader who inspires others to follow you and help them achieve their maximum potential? People need leaders, not taskmasters, Brad. Taskmasters are everywhere, in every organization. People look for leaders to provide guidance, support, direction, vision and the kind of relationship that empowers them to add real value to an organization. Above all, people need to feel valued."

"Okay, okay, I get it. I'm just saying a talking frog is just a little too much to swallow!"

"Remember, Brad, you're the one who told me you were clueless. Stay with me and it will all make sense. I promise."

"Call me crazy, but alright. I guess I'm in your hands."

"Good, because I put myself totally in the hands of a frog and it was the best thing I ever did for my career. In fact, it was the best thing I ever did for my life, work, family, friends and community.

I am who I am because of a frog."

"Wow!" exclaimed Brad. "I don't know if I've ever seen you so passionate."

"Leadership does require passion," Mike said with conviction.

Mike then looked out the window at the parking lot and back to Brad. "Except for my wife and family, I've never been more passionate about anything in my life. I look at that parking lot every day to remind myself of the lessons I learned at the pond. What I experienced there changed my life. The question is, will you let it change yours?"

Brad looked at Mike with a sheepish grin and said, "Sorry, Mike. From now on, Bob is as real to me as you are."

"Thanks, Brad. This journey you and I are about to take will be a reflection of the one Bob and I took. And keep this in mind; whether the lessons come from your friend, a classroom, or even a talking frog, it's the results that matter. So, hold onto your seat. Here we go."

After we introduced ourselves Bob began with a question. "I've been thinking about you all week. It's hard to think about anything else when a human is acting as strangely as you were. I knew what you were trying to do but couldn't do anything to respond. Why do you think it took you so many attempts before we were able to communicate?"

"I don't know," I responded. "I guess you didn't like the food I was trying to give you."

"Well, that's true," said Bob. "We don't eat old dead flies or processed frog food, but the food wasn't the issue. I think it was your behavior that prevented us from communicating. Think for a moment about what you were trying to do."

"Okay, I was trying to get you to trust me."

"Yes, but what you were really doing was attempting to bribe me. You may not have thought of it that way, but from my perspective it was a bribe. You can't manipulate trust. You see how it failed? If you want to develop a relationship of trust with anyone, you have to be completely transparent. If they think you have ulterior motives, you're toast. What do you feel changed to make me trust you?"

"I quit trying to give you something and started talking to you?" I asked.

"Good. Now, think about what you were saying to me. Do you remember?"

"I was frustrated. You wouldn't respond to anything I offered. In my frustration, I couldn't think of anything else to do, so I opened up and just started saying what was on my mind. I took a risk and spoke to a frog."

"Exactly! Even though I couldn't understand a word you were saying, I could see and feel that you were being honest and sincere about your intentions. That's when I knew you weren't trying to manipulate or bribe me. You were genuine. That led me to trust you enough to take a risk and talk to a human."

Bob's tongue shot out and grabbed a passing fly. He swallowed and then continued, "I have to admit, it does sound crazy. But this is the first lesson. When two people—or in our case, a person and a frog—want to communicate, it is vital that both parties stop, listen, observe, act, and be honest with each other. Then you can begin to understand what the other one has to offer."

"Yes, I can see that now," I replied. "Good point, Bob."

"Now that we have built some trust in each other, we can move forward. The key for us will be maintaining and strengthening trust throughout our relationship. What I have learned has allowed me to be successful with other frogs. Everything we do from now on will either build more trust or take trust away."

I nodded my head in agreement.

With a somewhat serious look on his face, Bob looked at me and asked, "Why do you want to be a leader?"

I chewed on that for a moment and replied, "I want to do a good job." I thought that was a pretty good answer, but Bob evidently didn't see it that way.

"Wanting to do a good job and being a leader are two completely different things!" he responded in some frustration. "In my world, any lead frog, or manager in your case, can do a good job if you're simply measuring success in terms of tasks accomplished. What's your real motivation to be a leader?"

I took my time answering the question. After some reflection I looked directly at Bob and said, "I want to make a difference. I want the people I lead to develop their full potential. And I want to build something that will last beyond myself."

Bob leaned back a little and broke into a big smile. "That's what leadership is about—encouraging people to exceed their own potential and to exceed the organization's expectations. Your people and the organization are better because of your efforts, and you will have made a positive and lasting impression on the people and the organization as a whole."

Bob waited a moment, so I could let it all sink in. "Mike, do you see how you have to learn to think right in order to have a positive impact on the lives of the people you lead? If your motivations are to truly help and inspire others, then your thinking must go way beyond yourself and the present moment. Leaders create cultures where people work together, feel safe to voice opinions, give suggestions, take risks, and plan for the future of the organization. Simply, leaders put the welfare of the people they lead before their own progression."

I nodded. It made sense.

"In the pond," continued Bob, "I'm constantly looking for frogs that can replace me. In our world we deal with the threat of predators, so I never know how long I'll be the leader sitting on the lily pad. In your world you never know what's going to happen so you have to think long-term as well. You will always be teaching and preparing your people."

"Yes, I see that," I replied. "I had a boss once who got the flu and was out for three weeks. None of the rest of us felt like we had the authority or ability to make the decisions he usually made. Things were a bit of a mess by the time he came back to work."

"Exactly! That's our goal—to have others trained to step up when needed. To create this type of atmosphere in the workplace, leadership requires a foundation of correct thinking and values. The leader's first decision is which values will govern his actions. Core values always determine the type of leader a person becomes. In my little pond, the values most important to me are *respect, integrity* and *loyalty*. I call them the Values of the Pond."

Building Trust

- *Leaders build trust*

- *Leaders develop people*

- *Leaders make a difference*

4

Values of the Pond

Wait, wait, wait!" Brad interrupted. "I'm willing to believe that all animals, frogs included, might have a hierarchy of values. Well, maybe no values, but some sort of built-in instinct that influences their behaviors the way that values influence our behaviors. But they're frogs! Wouldn't their most important instincts be something like survival? Or continuation of the species?"

"That's what I thought, as well," replied Mike. "But once I accepted a talking frog, I decided I might as well go all in. It's not that far of a leap from a talking frog to a frog who talks about business values."

Brad stared at Mike for a moment, then shrugged. "Fine. By the way, I see what you did there. Leap. Ha-ha."

Mike ignored the sarcasm and continued with his story.

Bob had just told me that values were important and given me his three most important ones: respect, integrity, and loyalty. But I had to ask, "Why only three values? Why these three? There are so many you could choose from. It sounds way too simplistic to me."

"Well you asked!" Bob said. "So, I'll answer. Based on what we just talked about a few minutes ago I'd like you to stop, listen, observe, and act upon what I'm about to tell you. Frogs value trust more than anything. The Values of the Pond have enabled me to gain and maintain the trust of most of the frogs in the pond."

"Okay," I said. "I'm willing."

"Values are the underpinnings of our lives. They form the basis for all of our beliefs and actions. While there are many values we personally adhere to, to be an effective leader you absolutely must incorporate these three essential values."

Bob paused a moment and gave me a piercing look, so I nodded in agreement. I had to give the guy credit. He really wanted me to understand what he was teaching me.

"The Values of the Pond are also the foundation of highly successful relationships. When leaders embrace and incorporate them into their leadership efforts, others are assured of reliable consistency in how they are treated by the leader. These Values establish, build, and maintain trust. A leader's effectiveness is directly related to the level of trust in the relationship."

At this point, I reached into my shirt pocket and pulled out a little notepad and pen. I could tell it was going to get interesting and I wanted to remember all of it.

"Let's begin with the first value: *respect*. Many people define respect as treating others as you would like to be treated. However, true respect means treating others how *they* would like to be treated, not as you think they should be treated. It requires a lot of work to discover how people want to be treated by you. You have to get to know them and actually care about what's important to them."

"Yes, I believe my wife and I have had discussions on that concept," I chuckled.

"Me, too."

"You have a wife?" I asked before thinking it through. It just popped out.

Bob didn't even bother responding, he just continued on as if I hadn't commented. "There are two kinds of respect: first, respect for qualities, traits, or accomplishments; and second, respect for the individual."

I nodded as I jotted that in my notepad.

"Let's look at the first one. The respect for qualities, traits, or accomplishments is what we call *earned respect*. We value the traits an individual possesses, their talents, contributions, and achievements. It's good and appropriate to show respect for these things. It shows we acknowledge who people are and what they have done. But this type of respect can be lost. Accomplishments are forgotten and talents may become obsolete."

"I see that a lot in our society, especially as people age. It makes me sad," I said.

"It happens with frogs, too. This earned respect can also be lost when individuals act in ways that are contrary to our or their values. But while respect for qualities, traits, or accomplishments can be lost due to an individual's actions, the right of an individual to be treated in a respectful manner should always be present."

"That's the second type, right?" I asked.

"Yes. This is often called *unearned or inherent respect*. Every individual has the right to receive respect, simply because they exist. In the workplace, it is the leader's responsibility to be respectful to the individual in every interaction. This right is an inherent right for all people, and frogs. In other words, the leader has a responsibility to demonstrate respect regardless of what they may think of the individual."

"Sort of the live and let live philosophy?" I asked.

"Sort of. Everyone has the right to have and express their thoughts and opinions and to be treated with respect all of the time, not just when we agree with them. The leader does not have the luxury to pick and choose when and how to respect others. Respect should be present in everything the leader says and does. Simply put, respect is not an option—it's a requirement."

"I like that."

"It's difficult to do sometimes, I'll admit. There are a few frogs around here that rub me the wrong way. But a leader must show respect, before they can expect to receive it from others. I overheard a conversation near the pond a little while ago. I know it works with frogs and I'm quite sure it works with humans, too. One of the frog leaders that I really admire said, *'Show respect even to frogs who don't deserve it, not as a reflection of their character, but as a reflection of yours.'* It's as simple as that, Mike. Leaders have character."

"Character. That was a big deal for my parents, and for me, too," I said.

"And it's a great lead-in to the next value, integrity."

Bob jumped right in to the next value. "Leaders with integrity demonstrate their values through behaviors that are consistent and reliable. There is a direct correlation between what a leader thinks and what a leader says and does. Integrity creates stability so others can trust the leader's intentions to do what they say they will do."

"I've heard it said like this, Integrity is doing the right thing—even when no one is watching," I added.

"Yes," replied Bob. "Words and actions are the outward manifestation of your values. Frogs are always watching me to see if I am true to the Values of the Pond. I assume it's also true of you humans. The great challenge of real leadership, and of life itself, is to continually work at bringing our behaviors in line with our values. It's not something that just happens. It's a continual process you must work on until you are safely dead."

"Man, Bob, you're quite the philosopher!" I teased.

"Wait 'til I tell you about the importance of having fidelity to your values," Bob responded with a smile. "But I really do mean that part about working on it until you are safely dead. Leadership is a lifelong endeavor. It's the way you live your entire life."

"That's how it was with my uncle Max," I said. "He wasn't perfect, but he taught me to always keep reaching for what I know is best. You remind me a little of him."

"I'll take that as a compliment," said Bob. "Now, a question for you to consider. How do you feel when people let you down?"

"I really hate it. I feel disappointed and sometimes discouraged. Why do you ask?"

"I ask because, as bad as you feel when others let you down, your people will be even more let down if they believe you're a hypocrite. If you ask them to do things you wouldn't do, or if you say things you don't believe, you let them down in a big way. They need the assurance that you'll be consistent and reliable in all things, all of the time. You must have complete alignment and fidelity with your words and actions. If you don't have complete fidelity, there can be no trust."

Bob paused for a moment before continuing. I'm not sure if he was collecting his thoughts or waiting for me to finish taking notes, but when I stopped writing and looked up at him, he moved on to the next topic.

"Organizations and their employees struggle with issues of loyalty during difficult times. Each must survive—but at what cost? Every person's experience with an organization is different. How they react is a matter of personal discretion. When frogs face danger or disruption, our natural response is "save yourself" rather than to be loyal to each other. In my group, the frogs have learned that I won't give in to this. They trust that I will do what's best for all the frogs. They know I have their backs and I know they have mine. As a result, when a crisis hits, we think of our team first."

"I see team members who act like those other frogs all the time—you know, the ones that take off. It seems that as soon as something goes wrong, they throw someone else under the bus. It's discouraging, especially when you're the one under the bus!"

Bob shuddered a bit. I don't think he liked the bus analogy.

"Strong leadership promotes personal loyalty between the leader and the individual. In uncertain and changing times, personal loyalty becomes the anchor in which individuals can trust the leader to act in a manner that is both loyal to the organization and to the individual. When times are tough, the individual can depend on the leader's support, honesty, and fairness—no matter what the outcome."

"But how do you build that loyalty in a team?" I asked.

"This falls to the leader, as well. The leader should always be loyal to the team. How can a leader expect loyalty from team members if he or she doesn't show it to them first? This is difficult when there are major conflicts, personality clashes, and differences of opinions. And loyalty doesn't mean you can't let people go for poor performance or other issues. But it does mean you tried your very best to turn things around first. You don't quit just because you experience some rough seas in a relationship. Loyalty breeds enthusiasm, devotion and creativity; all necessary elements to the growth and survival of any organization."

"Speaking of loyalty," I interjected. "I memorized a saying given to me by Uncle Max. He quoted a guy by the name of Clarence Frances, who was once the Chairman of General Foods: *You can buy a man's time: you can buy his physical presence at a given place; you can even buy a measured number of his skilled muscular motions per hour. But you cannot buy enthusiasm... You cannot buy loyalty... You cannot buy the devotion of hearts, minds or souls. You must earn these.*"

"Words to live by, Mike. Remember when you tried to buy my trust? It works the same way with loyalty. You can't buy it.

My frogs trust me because I've shown them the respect, integrity and loyalty they deserve. I've received much more in return from them."

"I bet you have! I know I'm more likely to give my all to a leader who shows those values."

"As am I," said Bob. "That's a lot to think about, Mike. We have a lot more to cover and the Values of the Pond will be central when we discuss Leadership Roles and Behaviors. For now, I've got to get back to the pond. Are you available tomorrow morning?"

"I'll make sure I am! Same time, same lily pad?"

"Yep," he croaked. Then turned and dove into the pond.

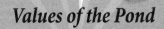

Values of the Pond

- Respect

- Integrity

- Loyalty

Introduction to
Leadership Behaviors

*T*o say that Brad was still questioning Mike's sanity was an understatement. It was all he could do to keep a respectful look on his face. This was a lot to take. Apparently Mike understood that, because he paused and waited for Brad to respond to what he'd shared.

"I just don't know what to say," said Brad.

"That's okay," said Mike. "As long as you're still willing to listen, I'm good. Should I continue?"

Brad nodded, confusion and doubt still in his eyes.

I met Bob the next morning at his lily pad. He was tapping his foot, as if he had been waiting anxiously to get on with the lessons. Before Bob could say anything, I spoke up and told him that after our discussion the previous day I'd had a chance to think more deeply about the Values of the Pond. I'd come to the same conclusion he had. He was right. The simple values of Respect, Integrity, and Loyalty did indeed encompass all the other values that are important to leadership in any organization, not just the pond. He nodded in agreement.

"I couldn't have asked for a better summary," Bob said. "Thanks for taking the time to think about the Values of the Pond. They are the foundation for dynamic leadership and should be incorporated into everything you say and do. Now that we have the Values of the Pond in place, I'd like to share with you the Behaviors and Roles of the Lily Pad. The Lily Pad is where our leaders sit and oversee the work."

"Your lily pad would be the same as my office."

"We have quite a few different names for things. You'll have to make the transition of what I teach you to your work and your leadership style, but the principles are the same. So, let's begin with the Behaviors."

I pulled out my notepad and pen, ready for another session of note-taking.

"There are a myriad of behaviors you will see in any organization, whether it be my pond or that gigantic building in which you work," said Bob. "Let me suggest, however, that there are specific behaviors that effective lead frogs, or leaders in your case, engage in that are essential to productive relationships. We're going to focus on eight specific behaviors."

I listed them as he spoke.

1. Empathic Listening
2. Gathering Information
3. Clarifying Information
4. Defining Expectations
5. Sharing Intentions
6. Exploring Options
7. Envisioning the Big Picture
8. Sponsoring Others

"Have you got all those, Mike?"

I nodded.

"Good. The purpose of each behavior is to provide a specific action you can take to engage one-on-one with those over whom you have stewardship. It's critical that you are genuine, sincere and always supportive when you engage in these behaviors. If used improperly, these behaviors can fall into the realm of manipulation. You can be sure your people will quickly catch on if you're trying to use them for your own benefit. You will instantly lose their trust."

"I don't want to do that!" I said.

"No good leader does. But if you're committed to the values of leadership and the vision of where you want to take your organization, these eight behaviors will be essential in getting there. Along our way we'll talk about behaviors, the roles of effective leaders, and how to work through any situation, no matter how tough, to a successful outcome. At the end, you will see how the core values of leadership drive not only your behaviors but also which roles you choose to take when helping your people reach their true potential. As you do this, your bottom line will take care of itself."

"That's good to hear because sometimes the bottom line becomes so overwhelming, it sucks the joy right out of the work."

"It does, indeed," Bob agreed. "Leaders lead—that's what they do. There are laws that govern success. As you align yourself to leadership values, behaviors, and roles, and interact appropriately with your people, they will perform. They'll feel needed and valued and motivated to work at their maximum potential to achieve the company's desired bottom line results."

Bob paused to look around at the other lily pads, something I noticed he did frequently during our chats. Apparently his frogs needed some attention. "Looks like we'll have to cut our lesson short today. I'm sorry, but work does interrupt sometimes. We accomplished quite a bit yesterday and today. Actually, we did something historic, a human talking to a frog. We've also learned the importance of trust and support, and that leaders are perpetual learners, no matter where that learning comes from. And we've also learned the Values of the Pond."

"Which are quickly becoming the values of my office, too."

Bob nodded and smiled. "I'll get back to my work, you go back to your office and each of us can think about how the Values of the Pond have an impact on trust levels, learning from any credible source, and being supportive of those you lead. We'll learn about the eight behaviors tomorrow. Same time?"

"That works for me."

I headed back to the building, turning my head back to the pond several times in disbelief at what had happened over the last two days. Each time I looked back at him, Bob would turn his head and look back at me. I'm sure he was thinking the same thing. Can humans and frogs really talk with each other?

Introduction to Leadership Behaviors

- Leaders are genuine
- Leaders are supportive
- Leaders align behaviors to values
- Behaviors produce actions, actions produce outcomes

Leadership Behaviors

W ell, Brad," said Mike, "that was my first couple of experiences with Bob. My hopes were high even though I felt crazy for talking to a frog. I went back to my office thinking about all it takes to become a leader."

"I have to admit, those were some great ideas," replied Brad.

"Can you imagine how stunned I was, when thirty minutes later, I sat at the boardroom table and the chairman announced the company had acquired the pond across the street near the office building? They were going to take the pond out to provide additional parking. Work was to begin in a few weeks."

"Oh, no! What did you do?" Brad caught himself and added, "I mean, assuming I decided to believe all this frog stuff, what did you do?"

"That's exactly what I was wondering, too! I sat in my chair at the table, paralyzed with shock and almost yelling in my mind, 'NOOOOOOOO! This can't be happening!' I certainly couldn't tell the chairman that less than an hour ago I had been talking to one of the frogs in that pond! I had plans to learn all about becoming one of his best leaders. How could they do this to me?"

Brad responded, "Well, there's nothing you can do. When the

big shots make a decision there's nothing we underlings can do. Is there?"

"Great question," answered Mike. "And I have a great answer. There's always something you can do, if you approach it the right way. Brad, Bob taught me that we are not just objects to be acted upon. We have the freedom to act for ourselves. Leaders act! Your sphere of influence is greater than you imagine. Bob and I worked together to solve that problem."

The entire night I worried about what was going to happen to the pond and the new relationship I had just begun with Bob. I kept asking myself what could be done to save the pond. It occurred to me that this was similar to what happens when one company acquires another. How could I stop the acquisition of my new found classroom? What would be the fate of the frogs and all the other creatures that lived in the pond? I didn't know if I should mention the company's plan to Bob or not. I was sure the news would create panic among the frogs.

I decided not to tell Bob at first. Maybe there was something I could do before I alarmed him. I didn't know what that was, but I wanted some time to think about my options.

The next day I hurried down to the pond. Bob was waiting on his lily pad. I tried to act as though nothing was wrong. He looked at me a minute longer than I expected, as if he were waiting for me to say something. I struggled, thinking maybe I should mention the company's plans, but stopped short of telling him. Instead, I said, "Let's go!"

"Okay," he said. "Did you think about our discussion from yesterday?"

He caught me by surprise. *That's right*, I thought. *I'm supposed to be thinking about trust, support, learning from different sources and the Values of the Pond.* "Well," I began, "I think everything we say and do should build trust between us."

"I feel the same way," he said. "Did you give some thought to how trust affects everything we do? How can we strengthen the trust we have established and how can we show support for each other?"

"That's an easy one," I said. "We should always be open and honest with each other, even if the information is hard to deliver or hard to take. We should rely on each other to be brutally honest. Also, we should trust one another to always be concerned about the other's best interests and show support, especially when the other one needs it most."

"Well said," Bob shot back. "We'll make it a rule to always do that, no matter what. How do you feel about that?"

"Agreed," I said.

"Okay," Bob said with some hesitation. He looked at me again for a few seconds as if he was waiting for me to say something else. When I didn't, he began. "Let's focus on the behaviors today. I mentioned there are eight specific behaviors that leaders need to know and use effectively. Do you have something to write with?"

"You bet. I brought my yellow notepad."

"Alright, try to keep up with me. Stop me anytime if you have questions or need some more time to write. Here are the eight behaviors again:

1. Empathic Listening
2. Gathering Information
3. Clarifying Information
4. Defining Expectations
5. Sharing Intentions
6. Exploring Options
7. Envisioning the Big Picture
8. Sponsoring Others

"I know they don't mean a lot to you yet, but together, they are powerful tools to work effectively with anyone. Each behavior has a unique purpose in the communication process and is essential for a successful relationship and to reach your desired outcomes. The first one, Empathic Listening, is the most important of all so we'll start there."

Leadership Behaviors

- Empathic Listening
- Gathering Information
- Clarifying
- Defining Expectations
- Sharing Intentions
- Exploring Options
- Envisioning
- Sponsoring

7

Empathic Listening

Did you get that list down in your notes, Brad?" Mike asked. "I know it's a long one but it's very important. Everything we discuss today will start with that list."

"Yes, I sure did," said Brad. "That was a very clear list and I'm looking forward to learning more about each of them. All of them made a certain kind of sense to me." He shook his head and added, "I mean, they make sense as long as I'm not remembering that it was a *frog's* list of leadership behaviors."

Mike laughed. "You're a good guy, Brad, to listen to all this. And believe me, I do know how you feel. After every meeting with Bob, I'd come back to the office and review my notes. They were great—but I was still worried about my sanity. I'm not at all offended by the fact that you're a little worried too."

"Well, unless that little green frog starts saying crazy stuff, I'm willing to keep listening."

"Before I was promoted to lead frog," said Bob, "I watched the other lead frogs, especially mine. They spent a great deal of time talking, giving orders, shouting directions, reprimanding, and telling us we weren't working hard enough."

"Sounds like some of the jobs I've worked," I said.

"It happens a lot, unfortunately. I knew I had a lot to contribute about how things were done around here, but no one would listen. So, I kept my mouth shut and just listened and observed. I didn't know it at the time, but that was one of the smartest things I've ever done. It's amazing the things you can learn by not talking."

"I'll have to remember that," I interrupted. "Oh, sorry. I suppose I should remember that right now!"

Bob chuckled. It's a good thing he didn't take offense easily.

"My lead frog got better results than the other lead frogs, but I felt we could do even better. When the rest of us frogs got together on our own time, we talked about how we would do things differently if we were lead frogs. There were actually some great ideas that came out of those discussions. Unfortunately, most lead frogs didn't care enough to listen. I decided if I were ever promoted I would spend a lot more time listening to my frogs and getting their input. And, that's exactly what I did when the promotion came. They talked. I listened. It was as simple as that. The difference was instant and amazing."

"I like that," I said. "I want to be a leader that listens to those on my team."

"The old adage, 'Frogs don't care how much you know until they know how much you care', is at the heart of Empathic Listening. It is not enough to just be quiet until the other person is finished talking. Not talking does not always mean we are actively listening."

"It doesn't?"

"Think about it for a minute. How many times are you thinking about your response while the other person is still talking?"

"More than I'd like to admit, I guess."

"Exactly," said Bob. "Empathic Listening means understanding the other person's message precisely as they intended. We must listen to the information, watch for the non-verbal cues, and tune into the emotions attached to the message. Remember, you are trying to understand the situation from the other person's perspective, not just your own."

"I can see that. I know I feel better when it seems like the other person is really hearing what I'm trying to say," I said. "I guess I've just never thought about how to do that."

"It takes some practice, but I'm sure you can get it. Just remember that people share information when the environment is accepting and safe. An individual will usually make an initial comment to get a feel for how the other person will respond. They are testing the waters to see if the other person will respect and value their input. If the response is not what they are looking for, he or she may not divulge additional information. The information they don't feel comfortable sharing may possibly be the critical piece to resolving the problem or issue."

I nodded. That really made a lot of sense.

"However, if the leader can tune into the 'message behind the message,' and demonstrate a willingness to receive additional information in an accepting and non-judgmental way, the other person will trust the leader enough to share further."

"I can think of many times that has been the case with my wife and myself. If it is valuable for us, I suppose it would be just as valuable in the workplace, too."

"Yes," said Bob. "Even more so simply because of the number of people you are communicating with. Empathic Listening establishes a foundation of trust allowing open, honest, and complete communication. Trust is accomplished when the leader demonstrates that the relationship is more important than the issue. Then the leader and individual can work together to peel away the layers of defensiveness and get to the true core of the problem."

"Trust. Honesty. Complete communication. That almost seems too simple to work," I said. I wondered if Bob somehow knew what I knew about the pond and if he was giving me this speech to encourage me to tell him. But I just didn't know if I could.

"Although this behavior seems quite simple," said Bob, "this is the one in which many leaders consistently fail. They fail because they don't try to understand the entire message. Leaders must learn to ask effective questions to bring out all the information. By doing so they can sort through information and come to a mutual understanding. This can allow them a better chance to solve problems, increase productivity, and look for creative ways to remain competitive. Empathic Listening requires real and focused effort on the part of the leader. Don't make assumptions. Confirming understanding will reduce the likelihood of confusion later on. Restate for correct understanding, get more specific information, and come to a consensus about what the information means."

Bob paused, again looking at me like he was waiting for me to say something. I was starting to feel more than a little nervous.

"I'll give you an example. I've been watching you this morning and noticed there is something not quite right. Your non-verbal cues don't match your words. You seem a little different from yesterday. You've said all the right things, but I sense there is something you haven't shared with me. Most people will either overlook the non-verbal cues or figure you will tell them when the time is right. However, an effective leader will deal with it immediately. It may or may not be critical, but you'll never know until the information is brought forward. The sooner a leader is aware of something and acts on it, the quicker it can be resolved. So, is there something you would like to tell me?"

"Boy, you sure are good," I said. Time to come clean. "Since you asked, I found out something yesterday that will affect you, me, and the entire pond. My boss announced they had purchased the pond and within a few weeks will be constructing a parking lot in its place. Everything in and around the pond will be destroyed. The news floored me, but I didn't want to alarm you until I had some time to think about what to do."

"So," Bob said somewhat sarcastically, "You didn't think that information was important enough to share immediately? You thought you could handle the situation better alone rather than letting us know about it? You realize that we're the ones that will be most affected by your company's decision?"

"Yes, but I didn't want to create a panic," I responded.

Bob gave me a pained look and said, "You thought we couldn't be trusted with the information—that we would panic? But you didn't think we would panic on the day construction began and there was nothing we could do about it?"

Stammering, I said. "I—I guess I didn't know what to say, so I didn't say anything."

"Mike," he said. "This is what I mean. Our relationship relies on a high level of trust where we share every relevant piece of information as soon as possible. That way we'll have the maximum amount of time to resolve things. I learned this in my own situation. I needed to first demonstrate to my frogs that I could be trusted with whatever they brought to me. We were a team and everyone's input was critical to the success of the team. Everyone in the organization, from top to bottom, has input and ideas that can help us improve. Empathic listening means we share information and listen to everyone, not just the people we think can handle it. Got it?"

"Loud and clear!" I said.

"It appears we have a pretty big problem facing us. Now that I know about it, let me process the information after we are done today. In the meantime, you know the meaning of Empathic Listening. Let me give you some pointers on how you can practice this behavior today at your work."

"Thank you! I guess I've proven I need the practice," I said.

"These are basic rules of thumb, and as with most frogs and probably humans, many will ignore them completely. If you want to be a good listener, you absolutely must do these things."

I set my pen on the notepad and said, "I'm ready!"

"First, keep and maintain eye contact. I don't mean you stare at them the entire time you're talking. That would be creepy. But looking at the individual during the conversation shows you care."

"Got it. Establish eye contact, but don't be a creeper."

Bob nodded. "Next, pay attention. Don't get distracted by what you want to say. Focus on what they are saying. Don't interrupt or try to finish their thoughts. Encourage them to share, ask for feelings, thoughts and ideas. Don't be afraid to ask for more information and make sure you are getting the entire message."

"Pay attention and get the message," I said.

"After they share with you, show sincere acceptance, both verbally and non-verbally. Be on the lookout when the words they are saying don't match up with their non-verbal cues. Let them know you aren't judging them or the information, but are trying to build a complete picture so that you can reach a positive and successful outcome together. Restate and summarize to clarify the information."

"Accept, restate and summarize. Oh, hey! That's what I just did." I glanced up at Bob and he gave me a big smile.

"Listen carefully and watch for body language that may indicate that this may be emotional or uncomfortable for the individual. It's okay for the leader to say, *It sounds like you are pretty upset.* Or, *This appears to be uncomfortable for you. Can you tell me what you are thinking?* Let people know it's fine to discuss what they're feeling."

Based on our earlier discussion when I was afraid to tell him about the pond, I knew he'd gotten that one right.

"Oh, and one more thing. I've noticed all of you humans have cell phones and other devices. There's no way you can listen with empathy if you have those things in front of you or if you are constantly checking them during a conversation. Get rid of anything that would keep you from being totally engaged with the person you are talking to."

"Hide cell phone." That one would be hard for me, but I was committed to practicing it at the office and at home.

"Now, I want you to practice this the rest of the day. Tomorrow we can discuss how you did. May I suggest you find an employee you don't have a good relationship with and practice Empathic Listening with them?"

Mike paused in his story telling, so Brad took advantage to interject. "Hey Mike. Can I interrupt for a second?"

"Sure." Mike replied. "Feel free to ask questions anytime. That's part of Empathic Listening."

"I want to be sure I understand you clearly. Are you saying we need to listen to everyone in all levels of the organization?"

"Absolutely," replied Mike. "Some people are afraid to do this because they feel threatened that someone will perceive them to be weak. Sometimes, because the other person has a lower rank, their viewpoint is considered insignificant. I've found it's the people doing the actual work who have some of the best ideas."

Brad was about to say something when there was a knock at the door.

"Come in," Mike said as the door opened. Terry, a part-time custodian, walked in.

"Hi, Terry, what can I help you with?" Mike asked.

"Hi, Mike." Terry shuffled a bit, then looked down at his feet. "I know it's late. Your secretary must have gone home and

I saw that your light was on. I don't want to interrupt something important."

Mike said, "Terry, you know you're welcome anytime and it's always a pleasure to talk with you. You're not interrupting at all! Brad and I were just taking a little break."

Terry took a deep breath and started. "I heard you got a promotion and you'll be moving upstairs. I wanted to take a moment to thank you for making me feel important, even though I'm only a part-time janitor."

"You are important," said Mike

"Yeah," Terry replied. "But you were the only one who said it and meant it. Remember when I was in your office a year or so ago, emptying your garbage and cleaning up? You called me by name and asked how things were going? I couldn't believe you knew my name, let alone asked me how I was doing."

Mike replied with a chuckle, "I have to admit, I knew your name because it was on your name tag!"

"That's true," said Terry. "But you were the only one who took the time to read it and address me as a person, not a janitor. I said that I was only a janitor and why would you care about my name? Then you asked me what would happen if I didn't empty your garbage or clean your office for three months. I said it would get pretty ripe in here in no time!"

The three men in the office laughed together at the thought of a ripe smelling office.

Terry continued. "That's why I'm here, to say thank you for treating me like I mattered. I may not get another chance to see you because I don't work on your new floor. Your acknowledgment meant everything to me. I hope you noticed that your garbage can was emptied twice as often and your office was cleaner than anyone else's."

"I sure did, Terry, and I should have said thank you more often." Mike said. "I hope you'll do the same for Brad now that he is taking over. In fact, Brad, this is Terry, one of the finest members of your team. I can promise you, Brad, if you take good care of Terry he'll take good care of you."

Looking directly at Terry and clasping his hand firmly, Mike said, "Terry, you don't know how much it means to me that you would take the time to express your gratitude and congratulations on my new assignment. I want to thank you for making my time here so pleasant. I enjoyed our conversations and I hope we will stay in touch. By the way, how is your son, Danny doing in football this year?"

"Great, he made first string guard on the offensive line. I'm very proud of him," he boasted as he picked up the garbage can and emptied it into a larger container.

"Me, too," said Mike as they shook hands. "Sure hope I see you around."

Terry left and Brad said, "I think you answered my question about listening to people at all levels of the organization. What I just saw was amazing! Now I know why I feel so important and valued when I'm with you. People really do matter to you, don't they?"

"Yes, they do," Mike said.

Empathic Listening

- Remove all distractions

- Focus on the individual

- Put aside personal agenda

- Take responsibility for personal mistakes

8

Practicing Empathic Listening

I think I'm getting it," said Brad. "People are important! It all boils down to that, doesn't it?"

"That's the sum of it. I've tried to learn the lessons taught to me by a frog and incorporate them in my personal acts of leadership," said Mike.

Brad looked at the time. "It's past hours, can we continue or do you have to leave?"

"Looks like you're my student now," Mike responded. "I have all the time in the world for you—within reason, of course. One of my favorite mantras is, 'You are not the interruption of my life, but the purpose for it.' It may sound cheesy, but it's made a big difference in how I work with people. Shall we go on with the story?"

I went back to work after talking with Bob. I thought of a couple of people I didn't know very well and decided to go out and talk with them. I had some interesting experiences, learning about their work, families, hobbies and concerns. Some were even brave enough to mention their fears and insecurities. I didn't give any counsel. I just listened, learned, and realized these conversations helped me appreciate the varying circumstances my employees faced each day they came to work. The real test, however, came the following morning.

Steve and Emily from Human Resources came to my office with what they perceived was a serious problem. Tony, one of our hourly employees on the factory floor, had filed a complaint against me stating I was passing him up for overtime work. They were quite concerned this might undermine my new position and create dissension and poor morale with my direct reports. Talk about an opportunity to practice Empathic Listening!

After meeting with Emily and Steve, I left my office to find Tony. It appeared he was waiting for me and he looked pretty mad. I went up to him and asked if he had some time to talk. I didn't want to talk in my office for fear others would think it was to reprimand him. But I also didn't want to talk where the other workers might overhear. I asked him to walk with me around the pond and he agreed.

I started at the opposite side of the pond from where I normally met with Bob. I didn't want him to see me fail at my attempt to reconcile this misunderstanding. This was an opportunity to practice Empathic Listening. I didn't know it then, but it was also a preparation for what I would learn the next day about the importance of Gathering and Clarifying Information.

Tony was quiet but I could see his clenched jaw and red splotches on the right side of his neck and near his temple. It looked like it was up to me to start the conversation. I was nervous and Tony was obviously mad. Not a good start for a productive chat. How do you start a non-contentious conversation under those circumstances?

Swallowing hard, I began as humbly as I could. "Tony, Steve and Emily from HR visited with me this morning about a complaint you filed concerning overtime. I can see you're upset about this and I'd like to talk about your complaint. I want to get your side of the story to see if we can work this out together."

Tony blasted me. "You bet I'm mad. You passed me up for overtime last Friday when I was next on the schedule! You knew I wanted as much overtime as I could get and you gave it to Bill, who wants overtime but doesn't need it, like me!"

By now, Tony's entire face was red and his voice was elevating. "This isn't the first time you passed me up either! That's why I filed the complaint. I've made it known to you on several occasions I would take all the overtime you could give me. What have you got against me?"

I was taken by complete surprise. This had escalated quickly from a written complaint to the point where Tony thought I had something personal against him. It seemed like it was getting worse, not better.

I decided to take Bob's advice to stay calm and keep listening. I didn't interrupt. I didn't try to offer any excuses. I just listened. It was painful and I could feel my heart start to pump. It was all I could do to control my own anger and frustration. But I shut my mouth, kept eye contact with Tony, and made sure my body language was open, not defensive.

I let him keep going until he had said what he wanted. After a half minute pause, I simply replied, "Tony, you're right. I apologize for not being a better listener. I mistakenly thought you were joking when you said in our meetings that you wanted all the overtime you could get. I wasn't paying as much attention as I should have. I'm listening now. What would you like me to do to resolve this?"

Tony looked like the proverbial deer caught in the headlights. You could see his entire demeanor go from anger and frustration to a calmer and more relaxed posture. He stammered for a few seconds and finally got out, "No one from management has ever talked to me like that. I thought you were going to offer me all kinds of phony excuses why you did what you did. I was expecting to talk to a company guy, not someone who actually cared."

I chuckled from sheer relief and said, "From what I'm hearing, I need to give you as much overtime as I can because of your personal situation. Is that right?"

"Yeah," he replied. "My daughter's in college and things are real tight right now. I wasn't as prepared as I thought I was and I'll need all the overtime I can manage. That would help my family tremendously. I may not be able to take it every time, but I would appreciate it if you offered it to me when it's my turn. I realize there are others who also need the overtime, too. I know I said it jokingly in our meetings, but I was hoping you'd get the message without me sounding desperate in front of the other employees."

I thought about what he'd said for a moment and then decided to take a chance. I realized I wasn't the only one at fault here. So, I asked him, "Tony, can you see how I got the wrong message? You assumed I would just figure out what you meant."

"Yeah, I could have been a lot better at communicating what I really needed," said Tony. "I didn't want to be embarrassed in front of the other workers."

"I can sure appreciate not wanting others to be aware of your personal situation. I don't know about you, Tony, but this has taught me a valuable lesson about saying what you mean and making sure we understand each other. From now on I will make sure to offer you every overtime opportunity I can when it comes up. Does that sound fair?"

"It sure does," said Tony.

"On the other side of the coin, will you try to be more clear when you need me to know something? That would really help me avoid making mistakes like this in the future."

Tony looked up at me and said, "I can see where I helped cause this problem. I'll work on being clearer when we talk."

"Tony, I'm very glad we had a chance to talk this over before this thing got way out of hand. Are there any other concerns we need to talk about?"

"No," he said. "Thanks for listening. I'm sorry I didn't come to you when I got so mad. You've proven to me that you're the kind of manager I can talk to. And, thanks for not chewing me out in front of everybody like our old boss used to do. I'll go to HR and withdraw the complaint. Also, I'll talk to Steve and Emily and let them know we've resolved the issue."

"Thanks, Tony. I'll follow up with them as well. I want to thank you for being honest with me and letting me know about an area I can work on. Will you do me a favor and let me know how I can improve in other areas? I'm new to this and I'm sure I'll make other mistakes. It's good to know someone is willing to tell me where the holes in my underwear are."

Tony and I both busted out laughing about that comment. I'm sure I could have said something a little more politically correct but I was just saying what I felt. I then said, "If we are okay and there's nothing more to talk about, I'm going to take another lap around the pond. I'll catch up with you later to make sure everything is okay. Thanks again, Tony."

Tony shook my hand and said, "Thank you for working through this problem with me. You've restored my faith in management."

Tony went back to work and I made my way over to Bob's lily pad. He was waiting for me.

"I see you're going to be a good student," Bob said. "I spotted you and the other guy walking to the other side of the pond, so I hopped over to the closest lily pad to listen. How do you think the conversation went?"

I told Bob I was extremely nervous at first, but it went a lot better than I expected.

"Why do you think it went better than expected?" he asked.

I thought for a moment. "I think it was because I didn't do all the talking and I actually listened to what Tony had to say. Plus, after I heard things from his perspective, I realized I shared a lot of the blame for the situation. If I had been listening to him with empathy from the start, we never would have had the problem. I should have observed his non-verbal message. Another good thing is that he took responsibility for his part as well. If we had communicated like this from the start it could have saved everybody involved a lot of trouble."

"Looks like the assignment to talk to someone found you, instead of the other way around," said Bob.

"Yeah, I guess so." I said. "Isn't that the way it so often works—you generally find what you are looking for. In this case trouble found me. It allowed me to practice my Empathic Listening skills in a pretty tough situation."

"What else do you think you could have done better?"

"Now that you mention it, I should have spent more time discussing why Tony felt he couldn't talk to me. I went too quickly and still don't completely understand why he was so quick to file a complaint rather than come to me personally."

"Well," said Bob, "It looks like you still have some more to do with Tony. But you're off to a great start. You know there are a couple more behaviors that will help you. They are gathering information and then clarifying that information. Those behaviors will help you become an even more effective listener. Are you available for more schooling tomorrow morning?"

"Yes I am. Today has been quite eye-opening and I've enjoyed what you've taught me. I look forward to tomorrow," Mike said as he turned and walked back to the office.

Practicing Empathic Listening

- Practice, practice, practice
- Evaluate the outcome
- Get feedback
- Try again

Gathering and Clarifying Information

T hat's an amazing example of Empathic Listening, Mike. It really helped me understand the concept," said Brad.

"I was grateful to have such an immediate situation where I could practice while it was still fresh in my mind. Not only did it help me understand empathic listening better, but I was even more excited to visit with Bob the next day."

The following morning, Bob and I sat in our usual places, me on the grass at the edge of the pond and Bob on his lily pad. School began.

"Gathering information requires we gather all the facts before acting or making decisions that can alter people's lives," said Bob. "There's never been a lily pad so thin there weren't two sides."

"Yeah." I said. "In my world we would say, 'There isn't a pancake or piece of cheese sliced so thin that there aren't two sides."

"Precisely!" Bob exclaimed. "We must be patient and consider all sides of any issue before making decisions that affect individuals or entire organizations. Take your time, let the dust settle, make sure of the facts in order to avoid knee jerk reactions that almost always hurt people."

"My dad always said the problem with knee-jerk reactions is you seem to always end up with your foot in your mouth."

Bob thought that was funny and did a quick pantomime of jerking his knee up.

"Where was I?" Bob asked. "Oh, yes. Leaders need to be tenacious about gathering information in order to compile all the facts of a situation. No one can expect a satisfactory resolution to a problem unless all of the information is uncovered. Different types of questions need to be asked: open-ended, closed-ended, reflective, and others are used to ensure as much information as possible is gathered."

"I know closed-ended questions are generally answered with yes or no, or some other very short answer. And open-ended questions require a longer response or an explanation. But I'm not sure I understand what a reflective question is," I said.

"Generally, those are the type that require some thought and critical analysis before answering," Bob replied. "Those types of questions are key to good communication because they elicit a deeper response. Let me emphasize again. Effective leaders are patient and do not make quick judgments or take action until all of the available information has been gathered. A snap decision based on incomplete information can create more problems than the original situation."

"I can see how reflective questions can really help gather good solid information," I said.

"Yes, they do. Just remember, when dealing with sensitive situations the leader must respectfully, yet thoroughly, probe for more information to ensure nothing has been left out. This prevents both the leader and individual from attempting to solve problems based on partial information. Gather all the information you can, then, clarify to make sure everyone has the same understanding of the facts. Which leads us to the next behavior, Clarifying Information."

"Clarifying Information. Does that mean you ask more questions to make something less confusing, to make it more clear?"

"Exactly," said Bob. "Once information has been gathered it must be sorted, understood, and agreed upon, or in other words, clarified. The object is to come to a mutual understanding of the situation at hand. The leader states how he or she understands the situation and provides an opportunity for the individual to do the same. Both parties need to see the matter from all sides and be willing to step away from their own position in order to look at it from the other person's perspective."

"Perspective," I said. "That's a great word. We sometimes talk about it as looking at the elephant from all sides."

"Us frogs do the same, only it's a dragonfly we're looking at. Clarifying information ensures that the relevant is sorted from the irrelevant. This avoids confusion about things like deadlines and performance requirements. The leader can feel confident that they and the individual have the same understanding so they can move forward from a commonly shared viewpoint. It's really quite simple. Before you act as a leader, make sure everyone is on board the same lily pad."

I laughed. "We say, on the same page."

"Same concept. I had no idea frogs and humans were so much alike," said Bob. "In order to be a truly effective listener, frog or human, you must be gathering information and clarifying all along the way. However, the behaviors have distinct functions. That's why we treat them separately. You will see later on when we talk about Leadership Roles how each behavior supports specific leadership activities related to each role."

A fly went buzzing by and I could tell Bob wanted to grab it, but he refrained.

"So, Mike. Do you have any questions about Gathering and Clarifying Information?"

"No," I replied. "I think I have it. I'm guessing you want me to go practice these behaviors before we talk next?"

"Yes, I do." Bob replied. "Here's how I want you to go about it. First, choose the one person on your team you know the least about. Without prying into personal matters, I want you to find out as much as you can about that person—their life, family, hobbies, and the things they are passionate about. You are looking for what makes them who they are. Remember to let them do most of the talking. Your job is to gather information and understand what they tell you. Then, do something."

"What do you mean, do something?" I asked.

"You'll figure it out," said Bob. "You'll know what to do if you have really practiced these behaviors."

"Okay," I said. "Sounds like an interesting challenge. Same time tomorrow?"

"Great," replied Bob. "See you then."

Gathering and Clarifying Information

- Let the dust settle

- Be patient

- Reach a mutual understanding

- Remember, there is your version, their version, and the truth

Practicing Gathering and Clarifying Information

Do something. That's the hard part," said Brad. "How do you know what to do? I mean, if you do the wrong thing, isn't that worse than doing anything at all?"

"I suppose in some cases it could be worse," said Mike. "A few times I have acted too soon on too little information and it muddied the waters, so to speak. But most of the time if you're sincere, even if your first attempt to change things isn't the best, the people you work with will cut you a little slack and let you try again."

"That's good to know," said Brad. "I just want to do this right!"

"I understand that. It's a sign of the good man that you are that you are worrying about this. And honestly, sometimes it doesn't work out the way you hope it will. But to create the best outcome, you need to practice gathering and clarifying information."

The next day I was waiting for Bob to show up. He was late. A few minutes later he surfaced from the pond and hopped onto the lily pad.

"Sorry," Bob said. "We've had a problem with the tadpoles getting out of their area. The older they get the more they want to explore! I guess I can't blame them."

Before Bob could say any more I blurted out. "You should have been there! I chose Jan as my practice subject. She's kind of older and pretty quiet so I haven't spent much time getting to know her."

"Hold on a minute," replied Bob. "Settle down and go a little slower. Start at the beginning."

"Sorry, I'm just excited about how my practice session went yesterday!" I almost shouted.

Bob gave me a slow smile. He could tell I was about to burst with the news.

"Jan is pretty quiet," I continued, "and since she's quite a bit older than me I didn't think we would have anything to talk about. But I remembered I wasn't there to do a lot of talking. So I put aside anything I wanted to say, asked questions and listened. It was a great experience! She told me about her career with our company. She has done so many things and has a much deeper background than I ever imagined."

"That's great!" said Bob.

"Then we talked about her family. I didn't know she was caring for her mother. She waits every day for her sister to come to the house so she can take over for Jan. That's why Jan is late to work so often. According to Jan, her sister isn't always reliable at showing up on time. She has four kids, twelve grandkids, she plays the piano..."

"I think I get the picture," interrupted Bob. "Can we go back to the part about Jan being late to work so much?"

"Oh, that's taken care of," I said. "I was going to call her into my office and have a stern talk with her about being to work on time. Not now."

"How come?" asked Bob.

I thought for a minute. "Well, remember when you told me to do something after I had listened to the other person? Jan and I worked out a solution to her problem of being late. We decided she can work a little later on the days she's late. This stuff is great!"

Then Bob asked, "How do you think your discussion would have gone with Jan if you hadn't taken the time to listen with empathy, to gather information, and to clarify what was communicated?"

"Not so good," I admitted. "I probably would have thought she was just making excuses for why she was always late. I wouldn't have been very flexible."

"That's right," said Bob. "Do you see that when you take time to listen with empathy, the other person is willing to share critical information? Then you start seeing things from their perspective."

"Yeah," I responded. "Another thing I learned was that Jan and I were developing a relationship. We were talking person to person, instead of boss to subordinate. I don't think she would have been so open with me if I'd started the conversation talking about her tardiness. Plus, we were able to prevent a little thing from escalating into a larger issue. We solved it quickly because I took the time to listen."

"You're doing very well!" Bob said. "From where I sit, I see several things. First, you took the time to ask genuine and sincere questions. You didn't make the mistake of turning a potential relationship-building exercise into an inquisition. If you truly want to develop a good relationship with others you must ask questions that will help them share because they want to, not because you asked. It's obvious you put yourself in Jan's shoes and tried to see things from her point of view. You asked good questions and clarified. You also demonstrated genuine concern for Jan. Do you see how important it is to develop and hone these behaviors?"

"You bet!" I exclaimed. "What do we learn next? I'm ready to get going."

Practicing Gathering and Clarifying Information

- *Define an issue*

- *Gather information*

- *Ask questions to clarify*

- *Evaluate and repeat, if needed*

Defining Expectations

*B*rad was really getting excited by this new information. It showed all over his face. "I'm ready to learn what's next too!" he exclaimed.

"Glad to see you're as excited to move forward as I was," said Mike. "But I don't want to move so fast that I overwhelm you. Are you sure you're ready for more?"

"You bet I am! I'm still a little leery about the whole frog thing, but assuming Bob is real, he's got great information," said Brad. "And, uh, I guess it's still great information even if he turns out to be a figment of your imagination."

"That's what I decided, too," said Mike.

Once again, Bob and I took our places in the makeshift classroom, Bob on his lily pad and me sitting by the edge of the pond, pencil at the ready. Bob began teaching.

"Mike, have you noticed that the first three behaviors are passive? By passive, I mean you aren't taking action but are preparing to act. You're setting the stage where you can now work toward achieving desired outcomes."

"Let me understand if I hear you right." I said, practicing my empathic listening and clarifying behaviors. "Are you saying that learning to listen empathically, gathering information, and then clarifying that information prepares the leader to act with confidence?"

"That's precisely what I'm saying," replied Bob. "It's been my experience that most frogs I work with, or in your case, people, have a fear of taking action and getting to work. The reason is usually because expectations haven't been clearly defined. Without clear direction they don't know what to do and their fear can become paralyzing."

"Oh, I am familiar with that! So many times after a meeting, I go back to my office to get started on the action tasks, only to realize I still have lots of questions and no idea where to start!"

"That happened to me a lot in my early days, before I became a lead frog. Too many leaders believe the best way to provide instruction or correction is to beat around the bush, so to speak. They mistakenly think this helps the message come across in a non-threatening or non-authoritative manner. The leader assumes the other person knows what they mean, and the other person assumes the leader shared all of their expectations. This failure to fully communicate creates most of the problems in the work environment. Here's a good example of something I did wrong not long ago…"

"What? You are still making mistakes?" I joked.

"Yes, Mike. I still make mistakes," replied Bob. He was totally unimpressed with my teasing. "I was trying to get one of my lead frogs to report on the maturation of the tadpoles in his section. I said, 'Gary, it's Wednesday. Would you please complete the tadpole report so I can review it for the frog council meeting on Friday afternoon?' What I meant was, 'Would you please have the report to me by ten o'clock tomorrow morning so I will have a full day to review the progress.'"

"Uh-oh. I think I can see where this is going," I said.

"You probably can. As Gary went about his business, doing everything but working on the report, I became increasingly irritated. When the report wasn't there on Thursday morning, I decided Gary was probably just busy. An hour later, I was a little perturbed that I didn't have the report. Two hours later, I started to get upset. By one o'clock, I was pretty angry, and by the end of the day I was ready to replace Gary. By the time Friday morning rolled around with no report I went over to Gary and began chewing him out for not doing his job."

"Oh, no," I chuckled. I did indeed know where this was going!

"I'll never forget his reply," Bob said with a sad smile. "'I did my job!' Gary said. 'Here's the report. My understanding was you wanted the report before your meeting this afternoon. Why are you mad at me? There's still three hours before your meeting. I did exactly what you told me to do!'"

"And he did," I said.

"Yes, he did exactly as I had instructed," Bob said. "That's when I realized the entire situation was my fault. I hadn't defined my expectations clearly enough. I didn't mention ten o'clock the next day, and I didn't tell him I wanted a full day to review the report. It's no wonder Gary didn't perform as I expected. If you look at it from his perspective, he not only did his job well, he got it done early! This one was on me. I also realized if I were going to keep my relationship with Gary and maintain my integrity, I had to admit that it was my fault."

"I see what you mean," I said. "I can think of a few times when I've done the same thing and blamed the employee when I didn't get the results I expected. Did you tell Gary it was your fault?"

"Of course," said Bob. "Gary thanked me for apologizing and told me he would have had it to me yesterday at ten, if that expectation had been clarified. He also admitted that maybe he could have asked me for more information, such as the specific time I needed the report. We both learned a valuable lesson that day. From then on I was very explicit about defining expectations and he was just as careful to clarify what I meant."

"Defining expectations and clarifying information. Who knew such a little thing could cause so much trouble when neglected!"

"True. The lesson I want you to learn, Mike, is that when leaders fail to define expectations clearly, the individual has less chance of getting it right. Ineffective leaders blame others when they don't get the desired results. Defining expectations in simple to understand terms and clarifying that the message has been understood, can avoid all kinds of problems. Success is easier to achieve when everyone knows exactly what is expected."

Defining Expectations

- Be supportive and direct

- Don't assume anything

- Come to mutual agreement on expectations

Practicing Defining Expectations

Mike paused from relating the story to Brad for a moment and leaned back in the leather chair. With his hands folded behind his head he asked, "How is all this sounding to you?"

Brad digested the question and said, "If I were Gary, I would have had the report sometime Friday afternoon, just like Bob said. If I were Bob, I would have gotten progressively mad because Gary didn't do what I asked. And if Bob had not taken responsibility for defining his expectations so poorly, the entire situation could have been blown out of proportion. Both parties would have been mad and the relationship would have been severely damaged."

"That's right," said Mike. "Can you think of any experiences you've had that might be similar?"

"You know, I can!" Brad answered. "This is the same problem I had with Howard in finance. I can see now that the problem was caused by me. I did a lousy job of defining expectations and I blamed him for not doing the job right. Looks like I owe him an apology."

"That's right," said Mike. "But only if your apology is sincere. You must also acknowledge you made a mistake and commit to defining expectations better in the future. Otherwise, your apology will be perceived as just another form of manipulation. Being genuine and sincere is essential to these behaviors."

The next day I met Bob at the pond. I was even more excited than the day before.

"Looks like you practiced your leadership behaviors," Bob said with a sly smile. Somehow he could always tell when I had good news to share.

"How do you know that?" I asked. More than once, I've wondered if this frog could read my mind.

"You appear more confident than before. Not so unsure of yourself as you were before," said Bob.

"Bob, you wouldn't believe the difference these few behaviors have made in such a short time!" I exclaimed.

"Try me," said Bob. "It happened to me, too! I saw immediate changes in the frogs I was working with. I saw changes in myself, too. Our communication was dramatically improved. My frogs weren't afraid to act because they knew exactly what was expected of them. Everyone's performance improved, things got done in time and, best of all, the quality of work exceeded even my own expectations!"

"The same thing is beginning to happen to me," I said to Bob. "I only had a couple of opportunities yesterday to practice, but let me tell you about them. In both situations I took my time and was careful to define expectations completely. Then, I gathered information and clarified to make sure we were both on the same page."

"And were you?" asked Bob.

"Yes! They left my office knowing exactly what was expected

of them."

"That's wonderful!"

"It's too early to tell the results," I said. "But both of the people left my office confident that they knew what to do and how to do it. And, I am very confident they'll both succeed. This is great stuff!"

"I agree, Mike," Bob said. "It looks like you're really getting the hang of it.

Practicing Defining Expectations

- *Evaluate a behavior that does not meet current expectations*

- *Listen, gather information, clarify*

- *Come to a mutual agreement*

- *Evaluate and repeat, if needed*

13

Sharing Intentions

Mike rocked forward in his chair and folded his hands in front of him on the desk. "How are you holding out, Brad? I'm good to go on, but are you? Or do you want to pick this up tomorrow?"

"No way!" exclaimed Brad. "This is all making sense to me. I'm willing to stay as long as it takes! I have a long way to go, but my fear of replacing you is starting to disappear. Tell me what Bob said next."

"His next lesson was about Sharing Intentions," said Mike.

The next time we met, Bob was eager to get started and jumped right into the next behavior. "Let's move on to Sharing Intentions. You will find this to be one of the most important in developing and maintaining relationships, as well as increasing your bottom line and productivity. Sharing intentions builds trust by creating a safe environment where you and your people are free to share information and express ideas, thoughts, and feelings without fear of negative repercussions. This type of freedom breeds confidence. Sharing intentions eliminates the culture of fear."

"You know, I see that culture of fear in many organizations," I said. "Too many of my friends are unhappy with their careers but don't feel they can talk about it with management for fear of being fired."

"Leaders have greater influence on the lives of the people who work for them than they realize," said Bob. "Because leaders have real and perceived power over individuals, everything they say and do has an enhanced meaning. It's easy for individuals to misinterpret, read more into messages, or blow things out of proportion when the leader does not disclose his or her intentions. This creates anxiety, mistrust, and defensiveness. They begin to wonder what the leader's true motives are. In my experience, when leaders share their intentions individuals will work harder, perform better, and deliver a higher quality result."

"I can see that. I know when I feel valued—as an employee, at my church, or even in my family—I tend to put more effort into what I do. I take more pride in my work."

"I do, too," said Bob. "Another reason for leaders to share their intentions is to create a trusting environment, where the individual doesn't feel threatened when things go wrong. Most people will think the worst unless the leader shares their intentions when working together to resolve issues. The individual needs to feel the leader's intentions are to help—not hurt."

"You know, that works for my kids, too," I said. "My son was having trouble getting to his football practices because our car was in the shop. The coach wasn't happy about it, and my son was afraid he'd be cut as a starter."

"That's exactly what I mean," said Bob. "Leaders must send a clear message that the relationship will continue in spite of the issues at hand. Another way to say it is, 'The relationship is more important than the issue.' We can work through this."

"And that's exactly what happened. After the second day, the coach pulled my son aside and asked what was going on. When he realized the problem wasn't my son's fault, he made arrangements to get him to practices until our car was fixed. He communicated to my son that he was a valuable asset to the team and they worked it out."

"I'm glad your son's coach practiced the behavior of sharing intentions," said Bob. "Here are some of the thoughts an individual may have regarding a leader's intentions when confidence and trust in the leader is low: *Are you trying to help me or hurt me? How much trouble am I in? Who can I get to share the blame? How can I defend myself? Is it safe to disclose certain information? Do you have another agenda I am not aware of? Am I being set up? What do you really think of me? Do you have my best interests in mind?*"

"That's just what my son was thinking before he had the chat with his coach."

"Sharing Intentions fosters collaboration by building trust, openness, and loyalty with the individual. A leader loses his or her effectiveness when people are afraid to share or express their ideas, especially when they differ from the leader. When trust is not present, the individual sees the leader as a boss or manager, not a leader. Remember, people choose to follow leaders because they inspire, lift, and encourage them. By sharing intentions effectively, the leader's vision is shared by everyone. They know exactly what the leader's intentions are and are more willing to unite in a common purpose. When this type of unity occurs organizations can really take off and rise above mediocrity."

Bob looked at me for several seconds, long enough that it became uncomfortable. Finally, he asked, "Are you keeping up with me?"

"I think so," I said. "Let me recap. If I share my intentions well enough that the other person knows I am trying to help them, not hurt them, they will be more willing to work with me to accomplish our desired outcome. Am I close?"

"You're getting it. This behavior requires some real practice before it comes naturally to you. More so than the other behaviors we have discussed. If you aren't genuine, your people will be suspicious of your real intentions. Since sharing intentions is mostly used when dealing with problems or difficult situations, your assignment is to find a person who is having a performance, commitment, or behavioral problem and share your intentions. That will allow him or her to understand you are there to help, not hinder or punish. Does anyone come to mind?"

"Let me think about that," I said. After a moment, I thought of some situations happening right then. "Two people come to mind. Both have expressed their unhappiness to other people that I got this position. They've made it clear that they were more qualified than me. Both have been with the company longer and they are good at their jobs. Maybe they have a legitimate complaint. I'll talk to them and see what happens."

"Alright," said Bob. "Mike, I'm pleased with your progress. It shows me you have a true desire to help the people you lead."

"Thanks, Bob." I said. "I really do. In fact, your comments remind me of a quote by Dale Carnegie that may apply here. It impressed me so much I memorized it."

> When dealing with people, let us remember we are not dealing with creatures of logic, we are dealing with creatures of emotion, creatures bristling with prejudices and motivated by pride and vanity... Any fool can criticize, condemn and complain—and most fools do.

> But it takes character and self-control to be understanding and forgiving.

"A great man shows his greatness,' said Carlyle,
'by the way he treats little men."

"You have a perfect example of this quote in the two people you are going to practice with," said Bob. "They are emotional about your promotion and they may have some prejudice toward you as a result. Remember, any fool can criticize, condemn, and complain. Make sure you aren't one of those fools. How can you be understanding and forgiving of them, and how are you going to get them to be fully invested in your team?"

"You're right. It's a tough situation but I'm confident we can turn it around. I'm going to let them know I am not mad or offended by their comments and that my intentions are to work together in a way that we can learn and progress. I can't wait to tell you all about it tomorrow."

"Good luck. I know you'll do great," Bob said. "See you tomorrow. You can report on your progress and then we'll discuss two more behaviors."

Sharing Intentions

- Create trust

- Eliminate culture of fear

- Reassure the intent is to help, not hurt

Practicing Sharing
Intentions

B rad couldn't wait for Mike to continue. "Well, how did the practice session go? Did you have the same success as the other sessions?"

"Not entirely," responded Mike. "I had a great experience with Kelli, but Nick was brutal."

"What made it so great with Kelli and so bad with Nick?"

"I'm not sure what happened, but I came out of it realizing I had some work to do around sharing intentions. I had thought by merely saying that I wanted to work together to resolve their anger, they would feel the same way. Kelli was on board right away. I guess Nick's experience with management in the past had left such a poor taste in his mouth that he wasn't willing to believe I was sincere."

"What did he do?" Brad asked.

"He just sat there with his arms folded, looking at the wall behind me," said Mike. "I bet he didn't make eye contact with me more than twice while we were talking. On the other hand, Kelli was more than appreciative that I was so open and honest with her. I had to laugh when she said that she was more qualified than me and she appreciated me recognizing that."

"I bet that broke the ice," said Brad.

"It certainly did!" replied Mike. "And there was no tension between us from that moment forward. But it took some time to break down some of Nick's walls. We never were buddies but we did manage to get along well enough to be productive. I learned you can't fix everything, but you can carve out a pathway to a working relationship that can benefit both parties. It was not the ideal I had hoped for, but there was enough unity to bring about positive results."

"What happened when you reported back to Bob?" asked Brad.

I looked Bob right in the eyes and said, "I failed."

Bob nodded and encouraged me to tell him what happened. After I'd rehearsed the positive experience with Kelli, and then the negative one with Nick, he had some great words of wisdom.

"Mike," he said, "We all experience less than ideal results sometimes. Even the best leaders cannot control the reactions of those they lead. We do the best we can and then let it go."

I sighed. I knew he was right.

"You are learning some significant lessons regarding leadership," Bob continued. "Leadership is often a lonely experience. Not everyone will respond the way you hope they will, so you have to find ways to make it happen. Remember, a good leader must strike a balance between bottom line and people. It's not as easy as it sounds."

I wasn't sure what Bob meant about leadership being lonely, but I did know this wouldn't be easy.

"Not everyone will buy into your style of leadership or your vision, Mike. You have to accept that. But that's what makes being a leader so exciting. There are a variety of situations you, as the leader, will need to figure out how to handle. Many people will appreciate an inclusive and participative style of leadership."

"What about those that don't?" I asked.

"It's up you to determine how to respond to those who choose not to follow you. Sometimes you have to dig pretty deep to stay calm and not get angry. It's their right to choose. It's important to accept that all isn't lost just because everyone doesn't resonate with your style of leadership. You still have to have confidence in the behaviors and learn to discern what role to use and how your values will impact your relationship with them."

Practicing Sharing Intentions

- Identify a misinterpreted intention

- Clearly share your intention

- Dig deep—practice and repeat, as needed

15

Exploring Options and Envisioning the Big Picture

Wow," said Brad. "That is pretty amazing stuff there. It's hard though, knowing that sometimes nothing you say or do is going to make a difference."

"Yes, it is," said Mike. "But I like to focus on the good stuff. This process has become even more amazing as time passes. Over the years, I've learned I have to do what is right and best for everyone involved, regardless of whether they like me or not. I found that my job is to get things done for the company while keeping people motivated, invested, and doing their best work."

"I can see that is an exciting challenge. I guess that's what makes the work interesting."

"Yep," replied Mike. "Bob had more to teach me that day. There are two more significant leadership behaviors, Exploring Options and Envisioning the Big Picture. Brad, do these terms sound familiar to you?"

"Of course," said Brad. "I've heard them from you and watched you in action. However, if you don't mind I'd like to hear about them right from the frog's mouth. So, tell me what Bob told you."

"Let's start with Exploring Options," said Bob. "A leader can be very influential by creating and supporting an environment in which options can be explored. This keeps the leader from steering the individual to specific solutions and making them feel like they are boxed in. When individuals feel boxed in, they may resist efforts for personal growth and improvement and revert to the primal instincts of fight or flight."

"I guess that's especially true for frogs," I said.

"It's more true for humans than you think, Mike," Bob replied. "They may not want to put forth the effort or improve in the ways you want. Neither of these is a desirable option when dealing with people in an organization. If they fight or resist, the problem is magnified. If they run away nothing is accomplished. You have only postponed the inevitable consequences that arise from not facing the situation. The leader provides access to information, the individual shares their ideas and suggestions, and together they open up all available possibilities. The individual can now make informed decisions regarding career planning, personal growth, and how they can contribute to the organization's goals. Everyone wins!"

"I like that," I said.

"Everyone likes to win! Exploring Options broadens the spectrum of choices by pushing for more information, encouraging flexibility, and reducing the pressure to 'do it the same old way.' The individual's ownership will increase when they have more control over the choices available to them. Leaders and individuals need to think outside the box to find options that may not normally be considered."

"So basically, you're saying that the more choices the team has, the more likely it is you'll create that win-win situation that everyone talks about?" I asked.

"You've got it!" said Bob. "Now, let's move on to Envisioning the Big Picture. Too many organizations fail to share information vital to the success of the individuals. People need to know where and how they and their work fit into the organization. They want to understand how to contribute in a meaningful way. They desire to know if the organization values them. This information is valuable to the employee in assessing just where they stand and the path they can carve out for themselves."

"It's like finding your spot in the big picture."

"Yes. Leaders will generally receive information about the company's direction and vision. Top management usually makes this a priority. Then it is the leader's job to effectively share this vision with those who do the work. Effective leaders should be willing to share whatever information is necessary to accomplish the goals of both the individual and the organization."

"Most people want opportunities to improve their skills and advance in their careers," I said. "I know I do."

"You're right," said Bob. "This is best accomplished when the individual's goals are aligned with the organization's goals. Leaders begin the envisioning process when they share the vision of the organization with those who will do the work. This vision helps people understand where the organization is going so they can set their own goals and choose opportunities to contribute. Envisioning also defines the parameters in which the individual must perform. This keeps their development and career goals in alignment with the organization's goals and maximizes their contributions."

"But how do you get the individual to cooperate?" I asked.

"Wise leaders will ask, 'What is your vision? What would you like to accomplish? What are your short-term and long-term goals? How can I help?'"

"And they will just tell you?"

"Usually," said Bob. "Especially if you have been practicing the behaviors we've already talked about, and have developed a level of trust with your team."

I think Bob could see that I was struggling with this. "Give it some time and let it happen," he said. "If you try to force improvements or skill building before they are ready, you are setting the stage for a letdown. People must progress at the rate with which they are comfortable or they will push back, and become less productive."

"I understand. I guess I'm just not sure how to determine if I'm pushing too hard."

"Effective leaders know their people and are aware of what the individuals are capable of, aspire to and want to achieve. You learned a lot about the people you work with when you practiced Empathic Listening, right?"

He was right. I had gotten to know several employees much better over the past few days. I was starting to feel a little more confident about the envisioning process.

"This awareness can help the leader envision avenues for the individual to achieve their goals at the same time that they are helping the organization achieve its goals. Remember, we're dealing with beings of emotion. Therefore, unfulfilled expectations almost always bring about negative results for the individual and the organization."

"You know, Mike," Brad interjected. "I resonate with what you just said. When I was working commercial construction to put myself through college, I would ask my foreman if I could look at the blueprints so I had a better idea of how my job fit into the project. I felt I could do a better job if I had a clearer understanding. He responded with, 'No way! Absolutely not! If I show you the blueprints, you'll know just as much as me!'"

"Do you realize how absurd that sounds now?" Mike asked.

"Yes! I kept doing my job the best I could but I never knew exactly *why* I was doing it. He never let me know when I was doing something right, but I sure heard about it when I didn't!"

"Can you see where he went wrong now?" asked Mike.

"I sure can," Brad answered, nodding his head vigorously.

"Here's a question for you, then. How did his behavior change your attitude about the job?"

"Well, it certainly wasn't the ideal work environment, but it paid the bills. Obviously, he didn't inspire me to pursue a career in construction." Brad paused and chuckled. "If every boss were like him, it would be a miserable way to make a living. On the other hand, if I'd had a better experience, things may have been different. I loved seeing something being built from the ground up to the final product. If he had been a better leader, instead of a supervisor, I may have had an entirely different career path and we wouldn't be sitting here talking today."

"Well, I'm sort of glad he wasn't a better leader, because I sure do like having you on my team," said Mike.

Brad nodded, then yawned. "Mike, I have to admit, as exciting as this is I'm having trouble keeping my eyes open."

"Yeah, me too," said Mike. "But this brings up one point not related to the behaviors but essential to being an effective leader. Make sure you leave time for yourself to recharge and reset. Spend time with your family and outside interests. Balancing your life is critical to maintaining your physical and emotional health. Plus, the time you spend at work and home will be far more productive and rewarding. We'll pick it up again in the morning."

"Thanks for sharing this with me Mike. It must have been difficult knowing that you couldn't share this story because people would think you were off your rocker."

"That's the reason I've never told anyone! It means a lot to me that you're willing to stay with me on this one. It does sound crazy but I promise you'll love the results."

Exploring and Envisioning

- Create environment where options can be explored

- Provide access to information

- Broaden the spectrum of choices

- Help others see their potential

Practicing Exploring and Envisioning

*T*he next day Brad went up to Mike's office to check out his 'new digs'.

"I was just on my way to see you," said Mike. "Now that you're here, do you mind if we continue in my office?"

"I was hoping you'd say that," Brad said. "I've already had a full day dealing with problems and it isn't even ten o'clock yet."

"What's going on?"

"Oh, just the usual quality issues. Nothing I can't handle, but it takes a lot of my time in meetings and one-on-ones. I needed time away to think about some of my next moves and I really wanted to hear how you practiced Exploring Options and Envisioning the Big Picture."

"Well, your timing couldn't have been better," said Mike. "Last night I was thinking about that. It took a little while for me to find the right time, but after meeting with Bob for a couple of weeks, a great opportunity showed up. You know how good the folks in payroll are, don't you?"

"You bet. Their motto is 'One mistake is one too many.'"

"Do you know how they came up with that motto?"

"I just assumed it was that way from the beginning."

"I wish! That's what I want to share with you. I was reading the monthly reports and noticed there was a defect rate in Payroll of close to ten percent. By any standards this was unacceptable. It had been the trend for quite a while, but no one was doing anything about it. When I asked the payroll manager, Roger, about it his response was, 'You can't be perfect all the time!'"

"Seriously? He said that?" asked Brad.

"Seriously. I almost lost it right there. But, then I remembered what Bob had been teaching me. I took my time and listened to Roger and his people. There was a general attitude that it didn't matter if they made little mistakes because they were only dealing with small amounts of money here and there. They believed that most people didn't really understand or even pay close attention to how payroll did their job."

"Unless their check is late," said Brad.

Mike laughed. "That's what they thought, but it's not correct. I had to use all the behaviors I'd learned from Bob as I worked with Roger. I needed to get him to see how important it was to be as completely accurate as possible. We discussed how small errors can lead to large consequences for people. When he finally saw the Big Picture, we then had to solve the problem in his entire department. He said that no one in his department realized how critical their function was in relationship to the organization and to all the personnel. Then he asked how we were going to get them on board."

"That is the golden question, isn't it?" asked Brad.

"You bet it is," said Mike. "We decided to bring the problem to their attention in a fun way. We created a short, entertaining but informative video. We showed a person whose taxes were improperly deducted from his paycheck being hauled off to prison for tax evasion. There was a woman about to retire who was going to receive a great deal less money from her retirement because her paperwork was filled out incorrectly. Overall, we had six examples of exaggerated, but severe, consequences and the impact their 'tiny' mistakes had on people and on the company."

"Did it work?"

"Yes, it did. After viewing the video, they all had a much better vision of how their work impacted the entire company. Then we brought them all together to explore options as to how they could improve the quality and accuracy of their work. The result was a dramatic increase in quality and a new motto: *One mistake is one too many.*"

"That's a great story, Mike. It gives me some good ideas about how to handle the problems I'm dealing with right now."

"It's one of my favorite stories to tell. Because of Bob, I have many more stories about how people's lives were positively influenced. That's the very best thing about becoming a good leader. Eventually, you get to see some great results."

Practicing Exploring/Envisioning

- Look for opportunities

- Ask for input and explore various options

- Envision and Share the Big Picture

- Practice as needed

17

Sponsoring Others

The next morning both Mike and Brad were busy so they scheduled a lunch meeting. Mike showed up holding two brown bags with sandwiches, chips, and sodas, and told Brad to follow him. They went out the side doors and into the parking lot that had replaced the pond. In one of the parking stalls near the far corner were two chairs and a table.

"I know what you're thinking," said Mike. "No, I haven't gone off the deep end. I have a good reason to eat lunch in this spot. You see, as far as I can calculate, directly under this table is where Bob's lily pad was located. I sat a couple of feet to the right, where this chair is. This is the exact spot I learned how to do what a leader does."

"It looks completely different now," said Brad.

"Yep, it does," said Mike as he looked around the parking lot. "But I want you to sit in this chair, close your eyes, and envision the pond as it used to be. Imagine yourself sitting on the grass at the pond's edge. Smell the flowers, the algae, the water. Listen to the sounds the frogs make as they go about their work. Listen to the other sounds around you—the birds, a gentle breeze blowing through the trees and ruffling leaves. Let your inhibitions go.

Don't worry about what people may think of you right now. Just try to see in your mind's eye today what I saw years ago in reality."

Brad sat in the chair with his eyes closed. Several people were leaving the building and walking toward the parking lot. They threw confused looks at Mike. When Brad heard the voices of the people walking by, he opened his eyes, forgetting the scene he had just imagined in his mind. He felt a little silly, as he looked around and recognized some of his own people watching them. Not knowing what to do, he flashed the two-fingered peace sign and smiled. *Yeah, I know, I do look pretty stupid sitting at a table with a sack lunch in the parking lot.*

"Hey, Brad," said Mike. "Are you feeling pretty stupid right now? You know, these people walking by and staring at us are the people you're supposed to be leading?"

"Well, yeah!" replied Brad. "Don't you feel stupid too? After all, we're in the middle of the parking lot, eating lunch while people are staring at us."

"That's the point of sitting here. When you lead, you can't worry about what everybody else thinks. You can't get distracted from your goals. The minute you do, you lose sight of what you're trying to accomplish. When you opened your eyes, what happened to the pond you had envisioned in your mind?"

"It vanished."

"Why do you think that happened?" asked Mike.

"Well, first, sitting here and imagining the pond is so far out of my comfort zone that I feel completely unsettled. And second, these people are going to think I'm crazy."

"I understand exactly what you're going through," said Mike. "All leaders have to go through the process of believing in their own vision and sticking to it. When you get distracted you lose your vision. Obviously, your vision will need to be flexible as you learn from those who do the work and from those who lead you. But the point is, *the leadership process never ends.* You must be an

attentive learner in order to become an informed leader. You can't
do that when you let others take you off course."

Brad looked at Mike, then looked around the parking lot,
noticing more people who were on his team, people who he
wanted to lead. He felt a great desire to be a good leader to them,
in the way that Mike had always been for him. "You're right, Mike.
You're absolutely right. Let's keep going."

"Great!" said Mike. "Let's go back to the vision you had before
you were distracted. Shut your eyes and let me know when you
want me to begin."

Brad closed his eyes again. It took several seconds to refocus.
Slowly, he started to see, hear, and smell what it might have been
like for Mike. He could see Mike, sitting on the edge of the pond,
being instructed by Bob. But this time he also saw Bob, two feet in
front of him, sitting on his lily pad.

"Wow!" Brad exclaimed. "I can see Bob!"

"That's wonderful," said Mike. "Now that you have the right
focus and you're envisioning what it was like for me, we can begin
the last behavior that Bob taught me. Continue to picture Bob
there on his lily pad, teaching me how to be a leader. Although we
are in the parking lot, stay at the pond's edge. Are you there?"

Brad closed his eyes and nodded that he was ready.

"Good. Envision yourself right there at the pond, learning
from the frog himself. Even though you are hearing my voice,
imagine that it's Bob speaking to you."

"The last Leadership Behavior is Sponsoring Others," said
Bob. "Leaders have the responsibility to sponsor the efforts of the
team and the individuals that are part of the team. Sponsoring
others is the action a leader takes for, and in behalf of, the team

members to help them develop strengths and overcome weaknesses. Smart leaders provide opportunities for their people to develop and grow, to overcome obstacles and weaknesses. They help them find different and exciting ways to use their talents and strengths to contribute to the organization. Effective Sponsoring enables individuals to push beyond their limitations and take risks without fear of failure or reprisal."

"How does that work?" I asked.

"Everyone has the ability to be an above-average performer. Every person can shine in his or her own way. A leader finds ways to make this happen. A leader gives public recognition and praise when their team or team members reach their goals and achieve success. A leader finds ways to let others in the organization know what the team members have achieved. It's common knowledge that people repeat and improve behaviors for which they are rewarded. Sponsoring reinforces exceptional performance so people are motivated to reach their full potential."

"Like when a team finishes a huge project and they go out for a team lunch?"

"That's one way," said Bob. "But there are many ways to recognize success. Some organizations tend to disregard, sometimes even punish people, instead of rewarding them. This can happen through simple neglect or sometimes it's built into the organizational barriers. It can come in the form of undue criticism, excessive regulations, personal biases, or bureaucratic barriers. An effective leader will be on the lookout for this and will try to remove or buffer obstacles their people encounter. Protecting your people inspires a high degree of loyalty that you can tap into as the relationship matures."

"My boss did that very thing!" I said. "Our team had worked so hard to hit a deadline a few months ago and no one said anything about it. Then my boss stepped up at the next company meeting and mentioned each one of us by name, noting the specific work we'd each participated in. When everyone applauded us, I felt really good."

"That's exactly what I mean by building up, protecting and looking out for your team," said Bob. "Managers sometimes try to protect their turf by keeping everyone else a notch or two below them. This is so counter-productive. I think they do this in an effort to appear irreplaceable or more important. But in reality, this is one of the quickest ways for organizations to fall behind the competition. People lose the motivation to work hard and succeed."

"Yeah," I said. "It was really hard to get going for a few days after we met that deadline. I was so tired and I felt like no one appreciated how hard we'd all worked."

"I'm glad you're recognizing these behaviors in your own experiences," said Bob. "The old crab metaphor, no matter how often it's repeated, is true. When crabs are in a boiling pot of water and one crab starts to climb out, the other crabs will grab it and pull it back. Everyone gets cooked! Leaders don't pull their people down, they boost them up. They act in everyone's best interests by bringing out the talents in people that contribute to the organization—even if they're better at some things than the leader. Inspirational leaders foster exceptional performance no matter where they find it. Again, everyone wins!"

"Wouldn't it be wonderful if all people performed at their peak potential without any expectation of a reward?" I asked.

"That would be ideal," said Bob, "but will that ever really happen? It most likely won't. That's why it's up to you to find ways to reward the good efforts of your team. Look for any opportunity to recognize and reward your people."

Mike looked at Brad and saw his eyes still closed. He hoped he wasn't asleep. "Are you still with me, Brad?"

"More than ever," said Brad as he opened his eyes. "I'm not sure I understand everything about the eight behaviors but I'm feeling more confident as I think about incorporating them into my own leadership style. I can see how the behaviors could actually work. I feel like I'm really learning, not just memorizing facts and theories."

Mike replied with enthusiasm. "I want to repeat something I said to you as we began these discussions. I have watched you over time. I know what you can do. That's the main reason I chose you to replace me. I see your potential and I have sponsored you for this position. What made me sure about it was when you admitted you were clueless, but willing to learn. Leaders at all levels must be continually willing to learn. The fact that you haven't tried to have me committed tells me our relationship is still on solid ground. Are you ready for a review?"

Brad sighed with relief, "That would be very helpful. I'm not sure I can keep it all straight."

Sponsoring Others

- Develop strengths

- Overcome weaknesses

- Protect those you lead

- Reward superior performance
  with opportunities

Practicing Sponsoring Others

Brad was relieved to have a short break and review some of the concepts he'd learned. It was easy for him to feel a little overwhelmed. While some of the basic principles were familiar, there was also a lot of brand new information to be absorbed. Mike was good at noticing when he needed these reviews.

"Before we head to the review," said Mike, "let me give you an example of Sponsoring. You can't just jump in and practice this behavior at any time, like you can with some of the others. With Sponsoring, you have to recognize the right time and place. This is one behavior you cannot force."

"I can see that some people would not appreciate you sticking your nose into their business," said Brad.

"It's all about the timing," said Mike. "Are you acquainted with Shaurelle, who runs the company cafeteria?"

"I haven't met her personally," Brad responded. "But I haven't seen a better run cafeteria anywhere. The people are great and the food is even better!"

"She worked for me in Accounts Receivable a few years ago."

"How did she get from there to running the cafeteria?"

"You won't believe it!" said Mike. "It's a good story. And not only does Shaurelle run the cafeteria, she's the reason we have it."

Brad looked at Mike, a little perplexed. "I still don't understand how it happened."

Mike laughed and began. "Shaurelle had worked for me for four years before coming into my office to give me her two week's notice and letter of resignation. When I asked her why, she responded that she couldn't stand working in Accounts Receivable any longer and she needed a change. This was a surprise to me because she always had a smile and her work was way above average."

"I'd guess that would have been a big surprise. Did she explain why?"

"Eventually," said Mike. "Rather than having a knee-jerk reaction to the shock of losing one of my finest employees, I decided to listen to what she had to say. I wanted to see if we could explore some options other than her resignation. During our conversation I learned she had been trained as a chef, had always loved cooking, and she wanted to pursue her passion rather than be stuck in a job she was good at but didn't enjoy."

"Wow! I can relate to that feeling."

"Many of us can. When your heart pulls one direction, but circumstances pull another, it can be frustrating. When Shaurelle was first married, they needed two full-time incomes to make it. But her husband was now making good enough money for her to find a job in the food industry. She'd have to start at the bottom but she figured she could work her way up in a few years. Sometimes fulfilling a dream is worth starting over."

"Yes, it is. How did you ever convince her to stay?"

"I encouraged her to tell me what her ideal job would be. She said she had always wanted to run a restaurant. She could cook anything and had been trained in restaurant management, but had no practical experience. She was well aware that it would take a lot of time and patience and low pay to get where she wanted to be, but she was willing to pay that price to do what she loved."

Mike shook his head. "I didn't know if anything I said or did could change her mind, but I knew she was too valuable to lose. I asked if she would be willing to explore some options. She agreed and after a few brainstorming sessions, this was the plan we came up with. She would work for me part time, and also find a part-time job at a restaurant where she could gain the experience she needed to run a restaurant."

"That sounds like a good compromise. You both got a little of what you wanted," said Brad.

"Yes," Mike said. "And in the meantime, my job was to sell the idea of a company cafeteria to the upper brass, with Shaurelle as the manager. I really had to go to bat for Shaurelle and to justify an on-site cafeteria. It took two years, but look at the results! Shaurelle loves what she is doing and she's making a huge contribution to the entire workforce of the company. Our productivity is better because so many people stay here for lunch to enjoy the great food rather than go out. They take shorter lunches and then get right back to work."

"Not to mention, she makes the best vegetarian lasagna I've ever tasted—and I'm a meat lover!" said Brad.

"I like that one too, which makes me doubly glad I worked so hard to keep Shaurelle," said Mike. "I didn't want to lose her as an employee, but at the same time, I wanted her to reach her full potential. Even though I lost her in Accounts Receivable, she is making a far more valuable contribution doing what she loves. We all have won. That's what Sponsoring Others is all about."

"That is what I want to do with those now under my charge," said Brad. "I want to help them reach their potential and create advantageous situations for both them *and* the company."

"Well, it won't always work out as well as it did with Shaurelle," said Mike, "but leaders never give up helping employees reach their full potential and doing what's best for them and their families."

Brad stared at his feet a long time before he raised his eyes to meet Mike's. "I wonder if any of our employees who regularly enjoy the benefits of the cafeteria have any idea that we almost lost not only Shaurelle, but might never have had a cafeteria that's second to none? All because you chose to sponsor her instead of just letting her go. That's a great story Mike. It also shows your humility because you never made it publicly known that you were the one responsible for all this. You let her receive the credit. I think I'm ready for that review now."

Practicing Sponsoring Others

- Develop strengths & overcome weaknesses for team members

- Look for opportunites to reward team members

- Evaluate and repeat, as needed

19

Leadership Behaviors Review

*B*rad, you haven't had the time to practice the behaviors like I did," said Mike. "And it did take practice. Don't worry if it takes some time to wrap your mind around these concepts. Even once you understand the concepts well, it will still take more time and practice for the behaviors to become second nature. The important thing is that you don't give up. You keep on practicing."

"I'll keep that in mind," said Brad.

"Try to envision one more time in your mind, Bob sitting on his lily pad and me sitting on the edge of the pond. As you do, take mental notes of how this can assist you to better understand the behaviors. Are you there yet?"

Brad closed his eyes again and replied, "Ready, let's go."

Bob looked at me and said, "Now I think you've got it, Mike. Let's find out which behaviors you feel most comfortable with and which ones may need more practice. We'll review each one briefly.

Please be honest with me and tell me where you need some clarification as we go through all eight."

"Okay," I said. "I can do that. But, I also ask you to be perfectly honest in your evaluation. I'm still a little fuzzy with a few of them."

"Agreed," said Bob. "Let's begin with Empathic Listening. How do you feel about this one?"

"This is one I definitely need to work on."

"How so?" asked Bob.

"I'm always trying to think about what I'm going to say next, rather than focusing on what the other person is saying. Sometimes it's difficult for me to put myself in another person's shoes in order to see their perspective."

Bob responded with sensitivity. "I've noticed that in you as well. It's difficult not to 'reload' while the other person is talking. I promise you, however, if you will continue practicing and being willing to surrender your agenda to the other person, you will capture the essence of empathic listening. You won't be nodding your head and pretending you are with them. You'll really be there."

"I hope so," I said.

"Here are a couple of things to remember. Keep your entire focus on the individual, not on your phone. Don't look out the window or at your to-do list. Don't let any other distraction creep in. You want to listen empathically, not superficially, so you can begin to see things as the other person sees them. Try to key into their non-verbal cues such as body language, facial expressions, pitch and emotions."

"Boy, I have a lot of work to do on empathic listening," I said with some exasperation.

"Most people do," said Bob. "But if you think you have a hard time of it, you should try communicating with another frog! They're the worst!"

I chuckled at that. "Well, I am communicating with a frog and he's pretty good."

Bob smiled and continued. "Okay, Gathering Information."

"I think I'm pretty good at gathering information."

"I agree," Bob responded. "But, let me give you a word of advice, don't become an interrogator. Use effective questions to get relevant information, but don't be intrusive."

"Great point!" I said with complete agreement.

Bob continued, "Moving on to Clarifying Information. How's this one for you?"

I responded with a positive tone. "I feel good about this one, too. I'm pretty straight forward, and that's always been an asset for me. I just don't want to be redundant. But I guess it's better to be sure everyone understands the same information, in the same way, rather than move forward with uncertainty."

"Sounds like you have that one down, too. What about Defining Expectations?" Bob asked.

"Well," I said, "I'm working on that one every day. I can see that I wasn't very good at it and that caused some real confusion for other people. Yet, as my ability to share intentions has improved, so has my ability to define expectations."

"Good point, Mike," Bob reflected. "Sharing Intentions is an art. Any art takes hard work to hone the skills of the craft. How you share your intentions will improve as you better learn to define your expectations to others. People feel more at ease because they know exactly where you're coming from."

"I have begun to notice that at the office," I said.

"Good," said Bob. "I hope you've noticed that the last three behaviors—Exploring Options, Envisioning the Big Picture, and Sponsoring Others are all related."

"I can see that now," I said. "When I envision the company's goals and how our division fits into those goals, we can more easily explore options on how to accomplish the goals. But I never thought of sponsoring as a leadership behavior until you mentioned it. I need to be better at sharing my vision in order for my team to understand where they fit and how they can contribute. I can show my support by sponsoring their efforts to improve and protect them from the other crabs in the pot that are always trying to pull them down."

"It looks to me like you have a fairly good understanding of these behaviors," said Bob. "However, it's important to remember that most people have a tendency to rely on two or three favorite behaviors. Generally, they rely on the behaviors with which they are most comfortable."

"Now that you mention it," I said, a little self-consciously. "I do have my top three favorites. Is that such a bad thing?"

"It can become a bad thing if you don't use the other behaviors as well. A leader might try a favorite behavior in the wrong situation. When that doesn't work they go to their next favorite behavior, and maybe a third. When that behavior doesn't get the desired results, you would think they would try one of the other eight behaviors. Instead, they go back and try their favorite behaviors all over again. Using the wrong behavior will never help things progress in a positive way. Can you see how that inhibits progress?"

"That's a great point. I never thought of it that way."

"It's a common mistake a lot of leaders make," Bob said. "They think their favorite behaviors will work in all situations. My hope for you is that you will become proficient in all eight behaviors. Different behaviors are needed in different situations and you can't rely on two or three alone. In fact, using the wrong behavior can impair what you are trying to accomplish."

"I see that," I replied. "I want to be effective so I must incorporate them all."

"That's correct," Bob said, nodding his head in agreement. "When we start talking about the Leadership Roles, you will see how each role requires specific behaviors. Not only that, but you must master each behavior in order to be effective in each role."

Brad opened his eyes and looked around at his surroundings. The parking lot was empty except for the two of them sitting at the table.

"Wow!" Brad exclaimed. "Great review. And, I wasn't distracted by everything around us. However, now I'm pretty hungry. We've been so focused on envisioning and story telling, we haven't touched our food."

"Let's pick everything up and get back to the office," Mike suggested. "These chairs aren't the most comfortable."

"Thanks," said Brad. "My feelings exactly."

Mike and Brad picked up the table and chairs and put them into the back of Mike's truck. Then, they took the uneaten sack lunches and walked back to Brad's office. Mike checked his watch and said, "I need to get back to work. Can we meet again at five o'clock and continue?"

"I'm kind of excited to get going. How about four o'clock?" Brad asked.

"I've got a lot to get done this afternoon and a meeting at four." Mike said.

"Okay, I'll be ready and waiting at five. See you then."

Leadership Behaviors Review

- Empathic Listening
- Gathering Information
- Clarifying
- Defining Expectations

- Sharing Intentions
- Exploring Options
- Envisioning
- Sponsoring

20

Saving the Pond

Mike walked into Brad's office a little after five o'clock
and sat in one of the side chairs across from Brad's
desk. Brad had been waiting impatiently for Mike to
arrive and simply said, "Let's get going. What happened after Bob
finished his review of the eight behaviors?"

Mike laughed and said, "Boy, you really are anxious to learn!
After my review, I went home, spent a relaxing evening with my
wife and children and prepared for my next meeting with Bob. I
struggled with the notion of telling my wife, Anne. In the end, I
decided to give it a few more days. It was still all too new. And to
be honest, Brad, I was afraid she wouldn't believe me."

"I can understand why you'd feel that way," said Brad. "I'm still
not sure I believe it. But I also can't deny that I've learned so much.
I'm eager to learn more."

The next morning, I went to the pond prior to going to my
office. The frogs were making their usual noises. As I approached

Bob, all of the frogs went silent. I could feel something like tension in the air.

Bob looked at me and simply said, "I told them. They're all hoping there's something you can do to help. It's completely out of our hands. I hate to say this but we are totally dependent on you for our homes, our work, and our lives."

I didn't know what to say, and I certainly had no idea what to do to help them. Bob could see I was at a loss.

"The only benefit we have is the forewarning," said Bob. "And we thank you for that. Otherwise, the machinery would have shown up one day and that would have been the end of us. This is a perfect example of why we all need to be completely open, honest, and willing to share important information. People's entire lives are upset if information is not shared and we are left in the dark. Looks like our entire world is in your hands now."

"Gee, thanks," I said. "I've actually been thinking about this since the meeting with the CEO. I've tried to figure out what kinds of actions I could take or who I could talk to. At this point I can't think of a thing I can do. I've checked with the EPA and looked at every document and procedure to see if there's anything I can do to stop or even stall this action. I hate to say this because it sounds so callous, but no living thing in this pond is considered an endangered species to us."

Bob slumped a little on his lily pad. I couldn't let this be the end of it. "Don't give up," I said. "I'm totally invested in you and this pond. Your saying, *Frogs Matter Most*, has much more meaning to me than I could have imagined. You have helped me so much, Bob. I wish I could get the leaders in my company to understand that it's the people who matter most. If they could figure out this one simple concept, bottom lines would increase, employee morale would skyrocket, turnover and dollars spent on training would decrease and the overall culture of the organization would improve."

I had hoped my words would lift Bob's spirit, but I could see that his worries about the pond and the other frogs were weighing him down. My heart really went out to him. I realized it wasn't just the business concepts I was learning that I valued—it was the pond and Bob himself. I couldn't believe how much I had come to love my time at this pond and talking to Bob, in such a short time. I was willing to do anything to help, if I just knew what.

"Seeing what my company's decision will do to every living creature in this pond has helped me realize what a critical situation does in the lives of people who aren't prepared for what awaits them. Bob, I'm truly sorry. I'll work as hard as I can to come up with something to save what you have so carefully built. Please let your frogs know that I'll be working in their behalf before the bulldozers get here. Whatever we come up with it will take a great deal of thought and work. When I return tomorrow I'll try to have some ideas. Hopefully, it will relieve some of the anxiety and hopelessness that you and the other frogs are feeling."

"Thank you, Mike," said Bob. "It means a great deal to me. I hate to think what would have happened to us if you and I hadn't found a way to communicate."

I let out my breath with a sigh. "I suppose I would have been an average leader at best, and you and your colony of frogs would have become extinct. It makes me think of an old saying by a superior leader in my life. He said, 'Decisions determine destiny.' I chose to talk with a frog and you chose to talk with a human. That is something neither of us would have done just a short time ago. Both of us have a great deal to be thankful for. Looks like we both made a great choice."

"I'm hoping you will have some good news for us tomorrow," Bob said, emotion evident in his voice. Then he gave a short croak and continued. "Until then, let's talk about Leadership Roles."

Saving the Pond

- People depend on their leaders

- Leaders have a greater influence than you think

- Do your homework

21

Leadership Roles

Brad stared at Mike. He couldn't believe it! He'd been certain they'd come up with some brilliant solution to the pond's problem. He was stunned that both Mike and Bob were at such a loss as to what to do. Even more, he was surprised at how upset he felt over a frog he still wasn't sure existed anywhere but in Mike's mind.

"What did you do? You must have found some kind of a solution, right?" he asked.

Mike just smiled. "Don't rush the story, Brad. Bob taught me some great new concepts about Leadership Roles that day, and that's what we're going to discuss now."

"Fine," agreed Brad. "As long as you promise to get back to the pond soon."

"I promise," said Mike.

I don't know how Bob was able to push his worries aside to talk about Leadership Roles, but he did—and I was grateful for it because it helped ease the worry for both of us. As Bob began to speak, the other frogs went back to their duties.

"Leaders engage in a variety of roles during the course of any given day. The role they engage in is largely determined by the performance and behaviors of the individuals they lead. Think of all the different roles a parent participates in—teacher, nurturer, encourager, supporter, provider, and disciplinarian, just to name a few. The intent in leadership is the same—to provide the proper leadership response to whatever situation arises."

I nodded. I had a couple of children by this time and it was true. I saw myself in many roles as a father.

"Understanding the various Leadership Roles will give you insight into which role provides the most effective response to the situation in front of you," Bob continued. "Learning these roles, how they relate to the performance or behavior of the individual, and when to engage in the roles, gives a leader great flexibility. The leader can then have greater influence on the outcome of any situation."

"I have learned that as a leader, flexibility is so important," I said. "Nothing ever seems to follow the original plan."

"That's right," said Bob. "Just like the behaviors we've discussed, you will find that you rely on the role that most closely matches your natural style. The key to success in leadership endeavors is to understand that all of the leadership roles are valuable. You need to be able to engage in the role that will be most effective.

"I hope there aren't too many of those roles, then, or I might find myself breaking up into a split personality!" I joked.

Bob laughed. I was glad to see him find the humor and hoped it helped him with his burden. "There are only four roles. Some leaders balk at this. They believe that having only four roles is over-simplifying. They expand the list of roles and then find themselves over-thinking things. That can lead to becoming overwhelmed and responding with raw emotion rather than using real skills that bring a positive result every time. I know it sounds simplistic, but when mastered, these four roles are the key to solving any leadership challenge.

Bob hopped onto the edge of the pond and with his right front foot drew a simple diagram in the mud. I made a quick sketch of it in my notepad.

"It's easy to see that two roles are above the line of the expected level of performance and two roles fall below the line. The line is going upward because you want the expected performance of the individual and the company to be continuously improving. Organizations can't afford to set the same goals year after year. Your competition isn't thinking that way. Leaders should expect that they will always be on the lookout for ways to do things faster, better, and more efficiently. Let's talk about the two roles that are below the line first."

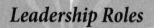

Leadership Roles

- *Coach*

- *Champion*

- *Counsel*

- *Provide*

Below the Line

ike grabbed a piece of paper and pencil from Brad's desk. He quickly sketched the diagram Bob had drawn for him.

"Counsel, Provide, Coach, Champion," Brad read aloud. "I'm not sure I would have listed any of those if someone had asked me to come up with four leadership roles. But I can see that those are great labels."

"Until I met Bob, my list might have been different, as well. More along the line of Supervisor, Discipliner, and the like," said Mike. "Thank goodness Bob taught me differently."

"The Provide and Counsel roles come into play when an individual's performance falls below the leader's expectations." Bob tapped the word Provide on the diagram with his front leg. "The Provide role is probably the least understood of all the leadership roles. The reason for this is two-fold. First, when the performance of the individual falls below the level of expectation, we naturally assume that it's the individual who needs fixing. This is not always the case. The second reason is that many leaders fail to completely comprehend the root causes of substandard performance."

I nodded. I clearly remembered times when it was completely my fault that someone on my team was falling short.

"Here are some things to look for to help you determine if the Provide role is necessary. The Provide role is engaged when:

- Performance is below expectations.
- Direction has been lost.
- New expectations need to be defined.
- Performance objectives need to be established, re-established or clarified.
- Movement is not in agreed upon direction.
- Developmental feedback is required.
- Conditions for the individual's success need to be discussed.

I had to write quickly to get all that down. This list was going to be vital!

"To put it simply," Bob said, "the individual desires to perform but needs something from the leader."

"So, what are you saying?" I asked. "Is this a situation where the individual wants to perform but doesn't have the right tools or training?"

"Precisely," Bob answered. "The purpose of the Provide role is to provide the individual with the things that are necessary for them to reach their goals. Too often we look at substandard performance and blame the individual. The truth is, in many cases the individual needs something from the leader or the organization, such as training, support, better tools, skill building, guidance, direction, defined expectations, or clearer goals, objectives and resources. When the individual receives the proper training, guidance, and resources, they will improve their performance until it meets or exceeds expectations."

"Now that I think of it, I've seen that happen so many times," I said. "I just never quite made the connection before."

"You'll see that connection more and more as you learn to act in this role. The important thing to remember when in the Provide role is that the individual *wants* to do a good job, but needs the leader to provide critical elements for their success. I believe most individuals possess the potential and desire to accomplish the results they have been hired to achieve. The company must have initially thought so because they hired the individual. Given proper guidance, direction, focus, resources, and support, they will meet expectations."

"I want to believe that will work, but sometimes I feel like it's just easier to do some of these jobs myself," I said.

"The leader's intent is not to do the work for the employee, but to provide clear direction and focus. The main objective is to define the task and performance objectives. In other words, to determine what needs to be done, and to provide the resources, skills, or support the individual needs to do it. They also need to identify the goals and factors for success. This can include discussing measures, strategies, and responsibilities. Once this has been accomplished and mutually understood, the leader needs to step out of the way, while demonstrating support and encouragement for the individual's performance."

"This gives the individual autonomy and empowerment in their job," I said. "Autonomy and empowerment are big buzz words right now."

"They are, and rightly so," said Bob. "There is a strong tendency for a leader to take too much control over the situation by over-managing and directing. You need to shed this traditional management behavior and let the empowerment process take place. This fosters personal accountability and self-confidence within the individual and strengthens trust and confidence within your relationship."

I nodded in agreement. "I hate it when I find myself micro-managing someone. It takes too much time and usually leaves both of us frustrated."

"Could you see me trying to hop from lily pad to lily pad, trying to manage all these frogs! I'd be exhausted by the end of the day!" Bob chuckled. "It helps me to remember that each of the roles has associated behaviors. The two primary behaviors that are most effective with the Provide role are Gathering Information and Defining Expectations. Can you guess why?"

"Let me try," I said. "In the Provide role, you want to gather information so you will understand what the individual needs in order to get back on track. You also want to be very specific when defining expectations so there won't be any question about which path to take to get the work accomplished. How's that?"

"You've got it!" Bob exclaimed. "The secondary behaviors are Empathic Listening, Clarifying Information, Sharing Intentions, and Envisioning the Big Picture. What do you think of that?"

"Hopefully, if I listen with empathy, it should be far easier to gather information, especially if the individual is self-conscious or embarrassed about their lack of skills, performance or under-standing. If I clarify, share my intentions, and envision properly, the person should see that my motives are to help them achieve the vision. Am I close?"

"Absolutely!" said Bob. "While we're on a roll and because I need to keep my mind off the pond, we'll cover the other three roles today as well. Are you up to it and do you have time?"

"Yes!" I replied. "I was so excited about being here today that I cleared my entire schedule this morning. I'm sure I'll have some explaining to do when people see me sitting at the pond all morning, but they'll get over it."

"Wow," said Brad, interrupting the story. "That's a lot of really great information. How were you able to absorb all of it?"

"Good notes," replied Mike. "And lots of practice."

"And then you jumped right into the next role? That must have been a really long day for you."

"It was, but very much worth every minute," said Mike. "Are you ready to jump back in?"

"Absolutely!"

"Okay," said Bob. "The next role below the line is Counsel. The Counsel role has been the typical management response when problems occur. Counseling is associated with poor performance and the discipline that is sure to follow. This role is used when:

- Performance is below expectations.
- Correctional feedback is required.
- Advising is needed .
- Performance or behavioral problems need to be solved.
- Conflict resolution needs to take place.

"You mean, when someone's in trouble?" I asked.

"I suppose that's a way of looking at it. The Counsel and Provide roles are similar, in that they both are used when an individual falls below the line of expected performance. The defining difference lies in the *attitude* of the individual. The individual who requires the Provide role wants to do a good job and meet expectations, but they need something from the leader or the organization in order to meet their objectives. When they get what they need, they perform. The Counsel role is needed when the individual has all they need to perform and they are capable of performing, but for some reason they choose not to perform."

"Ah, the slackers," I joked.

"Perhaps," said Bob. "But there can be other issues, as well. You have to remember they wanted this job or they wouldn't have applied. There's something else going on with them. The leader needs to define the problem and involve the individual in a productive discussion that will result in improved performance or changed behavior. Feedback and mutual problem solving is essential to correct the situation."

"Yes, you're right as usual, Bob. I have to admit that when I've really talked with people who I thought were just total goof-offs, I've found some underlying reason for their behavior."

"You'll find that to be true more often than not," said Bob. "Once again, the leader must avoid the traditional management traps of finding fault, blaming, or attacking the individual. Most people see the Counsel role as negative, both in context and outcome. However, it can be quickly turned into a very positive event when the appropriate behaviors are applied."

"That's good to know," I said. "Working with people who just don't seem to want to be there is difficult for me."

"The Leadership behaviors you have learned will help," said Bob. "The primary behaviors for the Counsel role are Empathic Listening, Defining Expectations, and Sharing Intentions. Okay Mike, why do you suppose these are the primary behaviors?"

"Okay, I got this one," I said. "The Counsel role can get pretty heated and emotions are going to be near the surface. Empathic Listening and Sharing Intentions will give the leader a chance to hear what the employee has to say, from their perspective, without judging or imposing consequences. Also, if the employee feels the leader is genuine and sincerely wants to hear all sides, it creates a trusting foundation for corrective action."

"That's right!" said Bob.

"Then once the leader and individual are on the same page, the leader will want to define expectations so all future efforts can be directed toward a positive outcome. Defining Expectations will be important, especially when the one being counseled doesn't think correction is necessary."

"Mike," Bob said with enthusiasm, "you're starting to think like a leader. You're beginning to see how the roles and behaviors work together for the benefit of everyone. And you're absolutely right! Because the Counsel role can be very emotional and sometimes sensitive, it requires a leader to focus on those three primary behaviors. But there are secondary behaviors that help in this role, as well."

"Secondary behaviors?" I asked.

"Yes," said Bob. "While not the main focus, these secondary set of behaviors are still very helpful and sometimes critical to the Counsel role. They are Gathering Information, Clarifying Information, and Exploring Options. Because the Counsel role can be so emotional or difficult to approach, you will need to use most of the leadership behaviors."

"I can see that this is a big role, and can get difficult at times," I said.

"Once the leader and the individual have agreed to move toward a positive solution there is still much to be done," said Bob. "Remember, you're dealing with creatures of emotion and the solution may be painful. Gather enough information to ensure you can move ahead with a comprehensive and workable plan. Clarify and Share Expectations, so both parties have the same vision of the outcome and are aware of all consequences. This way the individual can choose a path that suits them best."

"I do have to say that leadership isn't quite as easy as some people make it out to be," I said.

"You're right," Bob replied. "If it were easy, everyone would be doing it. That's not to say that there are those who can't do it. I think most people who want to learn solid leadership principles can be successful, whether they're leading in a family, a neighborhood event, a classroom, or in business. But look around your world. How many people do you think are exceptional leaders?"

"Not many," I said. "I see your point."

"Okay. Are you ready to address the two roles above the line? This is where leadership really gets fun!"

"I'm always ready for some fun!" I laughed.

Below the Line

- **Provide**
  Individual needs direction from leader

- **Counsel**
  Individual needs correction from leader

23

Above the Line

"Are you telling me you started right in on the next set of roles?" asked Brad, amazement clear on his face. "That was moving fast!"

"Well, not exactly," Mike answered. "We took a quick break. A frog on Bob's team interrupted and needed him to go help with something. I took advantage of the break and got a snack and some bottled water. But then we were right back at it."

"Okay, where were we?" asked Bob, when we were both settled back in our spots, he on his lily pad and me sitting near the edge of the pond.

"We're going above the line!"

"That's right. The role of a Coach is to reinforce and sustain positive performance and behaviors. Coaching is a positive activity because the leader is engaged in motivating, recognizing efforts and rewarding individuals. Engage in the Coach role when:

- Recognizing performance.

- Developing potential.
- Motivation is needed.
- Encouragement to sustain efforts is warranted.
- When challenging others for increased performance.

"The fun stuff?" I asked.

"Exactly. This role should be your dominant leadership role. In other words, this is where most of the leader's efforts should be concentrated. Most people perform at or above the line of expected performance. They deserve motivation, feedback, and recognition for their good work. Coaching acknowledges their efforts and challenges them to develop their skills further."

"This is the stuff we discussed when we talked about Sponsoring, right?"

"You're getting ahead of me, Mike," said Bob with a smile. "Leaders recognize the value of coaching and reinforcing the efforts of their people. Supporting, encouraging, and developing an individual pays huge dividends both to the organization and to the individual. As I mentioned earlier, look for ways to reward the people that work for you. Stay as upbeat and positive as you can, even when you are facing tough situations. Complaining about a situation only makes it worse. There are always actions you can take and something positive that can come from challenges. Look for the upside and you will usually find it. That sums up the Coach role."

"That's it?" I asked incredulously. "You say Coaching is the dominant role and the one in which we should be engaged most of the time, and that's all you have to say about it?"

"Think for a moment, Mike. You're dealing with people who are performing at or above expectations already. What kind of additional guidance do you feel they need?"

"Not much," I agreed.

"As a leader, what do you want them to do?" Bob asked.

"I guess I want them to keep doing what they're doing," I responded.

"Correct. Most people do their jobs pretty well. When things change or the company needs to improve, they improve, adapt, and continue doing their jobs. They know it and you know it. What they really need from you is to let them know that you know. They need coaching."

"Recognition," I said.

"Exactly," said Bob. "Recognize their efforts, show appreciation, and reward them. The only primary behavior for coaching is Envisioning. Why? When you show them the end goal and the path, they will typically find a way to get there. Show them the vision, get out of their way, cheer them on, and they'll get the job done. Secondary behaviors are Empathic Listening, Clarifying Information, Defining Expectations and Sharing Intentions. They serve to keep everyone focused and help to make little adjustments along the way to keep everyone on course."

"That sounds a lot more fun than the other roles you have taught me," I said. "In fact, my uncle Max used a fun term I always appreciated. He would say, 'Lead, don't snoopervise!'"

"I like that word, *snoopervise*," Bob exclaimed. "It sums up what we've been discussing about letting people do things their way. Most people appreciate autonomy. It's very difficult when someone is constantly looking over their shoulder."

"I always make more mistakes when someone is looking over my shoulder," I said.

"Most frogs do, too. I can only imagine it's the same with people. Too much *snoopervising* makes things worse, not better. But if you engage in the Provide and Counsel roles using the correct behaviors, you can quickly move into the Coach role as you see their performance improve. Any upward movement or improvement can be coached. Think of it this way. Right now you probably spend most of your time and worry on five to ten per-cent of your people. Those are the ones below the line, needing you to act in the Counsel role. Your job will be more positive and rewarding when you can coach your people instead of having to counsel them."

"You've got that right!" I said. "I can't wait until every one of my people only require me to act in the Coach role."

"Wait," Brad interrupted. "Is that a reasonable expectation? That no one will ever need you to act in the Counsel role? Tell me, honestly."

"Honestly, no," said Mike. "At least, not for an extended period of time. People change, circumstances change—and that often requires me to act as a Counselor, rather than a Coach. New hires sometimes need me to counsel, as well as provide. At least, for awhile. But I can honestly tell you, I spend much more of my time acting as a Coach now than I did before I met Bob."

"I can handle that," said Brad. "If most of my time was spent coaching, I suppose the time I needed to counsel would be more bearable."

"Indeed, it is," said Mike.

"What's left?" asked Brad. "It's hard to believe another role would be needed."

"That's exactly what I asked Bob," Mike replied.

"It looks to me like you've covered all scenarios with the three roles. What could the fourth role possibly be?" I asked.

"Good question," replied Bob. The final role is Champion. The Champion role serves a dual purpose—removing obstacles and barriers, and protecting the individual. This ensures that the organization has experienced and talented individuals and qualified leadership to meet the challenges of the future. You engage in the Champion role when:

- Achievements should be made public.
- Criticism needs to be diffused or redirected.
- Intercession on another's behalf is required.
- Obstacles or barriers need to be removed.

"Oh, we talked about this with Sponsoring, didn't we?"

Bob gave me a stern look and said, "Stop jumping ahead!" Then he laughed and continued. "Individuals deserve visibility. They deserve to be rewarded when warranted. They may need a little guidance, so as Champion you provide a vision for growth potential and let them become your superstars.

"Superstars?" I asked.

"Superstars are the individuals who are internally motivated to exceed established expectations. They don't care what standards you set, their desire is to exceed them. When the individual's goals are aligned with the organization's goals, this creates exciting possibilities for the leader as well as the individual."

"Can everyone be a superstar?"

"That is our hope. They can certainly all learn to be superstars, if they have the desire," said Bob. "When you see even a glimmer of that desire, you step up as Champion. When an individual has demonstrated a capability and willingness to receive additional responsibilities they should be publicly recognized and rewarded. They should also be given the chance to fulfill personal aspirations within the organization. A leader provides opportunities for the individual to demonstrate their talents in more responsible and challenging assignments. This is the group you will most likely look to for developing the next generation of leadership."

"I can see that having a pool of superstars to choose from would be helpful when you're looking to fill positions."

"Yes," said Bob. "But acting as a Champion is not just about recognition and cheerleading. It's also about protection. Think of it as being a knight in shining armor. The leader must sometimes intercede on behalf of the individual to protect them from unwarranted criticism. For example, when someone has aspirations to rise in the organization, others will be critical of them. In our world, they use the term frog-hopper."

"Oh, yeah, I think I understand," I said. "We have a few terms for that, like brown-noser, kiss-up, or even boot-licker."

Bob laughed. "It looks like you have more ways to be critical of a person than we do. But it's all the same. Many of the people who use those terms are just like the crabs in the pot trying to pull the other crabs back into the boiling water. You can't let that happen to your superstars."

"No, you can't."

"The individual who already knows and has exceeded expectations requires little direction. However, they still need support, protection, envisioning, and mentoring to achieve success. You can see why Sponsoring is the only primary behavior for the Champion role. Exploring Options and Sharing Intentions are the secondary behaviors."

"Yes, I see that."

"I do have a word of caution about superstars," said Bob. "While they are proven assets to the organization, the leader still needs to keep them focused within organizational boundaries. In addition, if they don't receive what they need from you in terms of recognition and chances to advance, they can quickly become frustrated or disillusioned. You may lose them when they leave to go where they will feel more valued, which gives your competition the value of their expertise and experience. Even worse, they may turn their once productive motivations into destructive behaviors that can negatively affect everyone."

"So you're saying that high turnover and inter-office conflict are signs that the leaders are not acting as Champions? I bet that's when you go back to acting in the roles of Counsel and Coach until it's resolved."

"Absolutely! Put a gold star on your forehead and move to the head of the class!"

Above the Line

- **Coach**
  Recognize, develop, motivate

- **Champion**
  Protect, sponsor, provide opportunities

24

Making it Real

Gold star," laughed Brad. "I see what he did there. He was being a Champion."

"Yes, he was," said Mike. "Some times a few encouraging words are all it takes. Are you ready to move forward?"

"Go for it," said Brad.

"Mike, do you have any thoughts or concerns about what you have learned so far?"

"Well, Bob. It's a lot to think about, but everything is fitting into a nice pattern for me. I can see that it's important to practice each of the behaviors and learn how they fit into the roles. As I have practiced the behaviors, I can see the need to be very proficient in each of them. Especially when dealing with different people in different situations. It's almost like each behavior will phase into another one and back again depending on the conversation."

"Yes, you need to be comfortable engaging in each of the behaviors and roles. Your goal is to be seamless as you do.

Remember, each behavior has a specific purpose to move people in a positive direction."

"Okay, I'm good on that point," I said. "Here's my concern. Someday I'll feel more confident and proficient with all eight behaviors. What's to stop me from using them to manipulate people so they'll do what I want? One of my old bosses once told me that the essence of leadership is the ability to fake sincerity."

"How did that work for your old boss?" asked Bob.

"He thought he was fooling us, but everyone knew he was faking it," I answered. "Plus, no one had any of respect for him because we all knew he wasn't genuine. We didn't feel he had real respect for us either. We certainly didn't put forth our best efforts for him. I guess you could say it didn't work very well for him."

"You know, that's a perfect example of what we discussed at the beginning. Remember our talk about respect and support?"

"You said a leader should always show respect and support for the people he or she leads."

"That's right," said Bob. "You can show respect and support in several ways—through the things you say, how you say them, and the things you do. Even your facial expressions and body language show respect, or lack of it. People can always tell when you're faking it by the way your interactions make them feel. You may be able to fake it during one conversation but no one can fake it throughout an entire relationship. And that's what we're talking about, developing and maintaining effective and productive relationships with the people you lead."

"I believe that," I said. "I was reading an article the other day and came across a quote I liked. I happened to put it in my notebook. Harry B. Thayer, the founder of AT&T—that's a big company here among the humans—said, *'It is easy to fool yourself, it is possible to fool the people you work for. It is more difficult to fool the people you work with. But it is almost impossible to fool the people who work under you.'*"

"I couldn't have said it better!" said Bob. "Leadership is a choice that should never be taken lightly. I have learned that what I say and do really matters to the frogs I lead. Not because I'm so brilliant and great, but because, as their leader, what I say and do has a greater impact on their lives than I ever thought. For that very reason, I am careful to use all of the behaviors. I lead because I care for every one of the frogs I work with. They follow because they know I care and can trust me to do what's best for them."

"Bob, I can't tell you how much I have learned in just a few short days. They sure don't teach this stuff in school, and they certainly don't teach you when you get promoted. In fact, I felt like I was left hanging in the wind. One day I was a regular person, doing my job, and the very next day I was supposed to be a leader."

"Yeah, the same thing happened to me," said Bob.

"How did you manage to learn what you did?" I asked.

"I was lucky," responded Bob. "I took over from a good frog. He didn't know how to teach me so I watched and learned. He did teach me one thing that I'll never forget."

"What's that?" I asked.

"He would always say, *Frogs Matter Most*. He never said much of anything else, just frogs matter most. The rest I figured out on my own. You'll also have to do some figuring out on your own, too. But with a good foundation you can do it."

"Thanks for the vote of confidence." I said. "Coming from you, it means a lot. I guess I have some figuring out to do tonight. I'm certain there's a solution about how to save the pond and all the frogs. After all, frogs really do matter most!"

Making It Real

- Frogs and people matter most

- Be genuine

- Don't manipulate

25

Putting It All Together and Taking Action

*L*earning about all those Leadership Roles made for a really, really a long day," said Mike.

"I can imagine. I bet you were exhausted," said Brad. "I feel a little exhausted myself—and I'm not talking to a frog!"

Mike laughed. "I was tired, that's for sure. But I was exhilarated too. After spending the rest of the day catching up at work, I finally made it home late that night."

"What did your wife say about that?"

"Unfortunately, she was used to my late evenings by that time," said Mike. "My mind was swimming with all the information we'd covered—about roles, behaviors, frogs, and ponds. I knew I needed to review what we'd talked about. But I was also worried about Bob's future. How was I going to save the frogs? My mind was just too full. I decided the best way to remember all Bob and I had discussed that morning was to put it into a diagram on a piece of paper."

Mike pulled a worn sheet of paper from his briefcase. "I made a spreadsheet," he said. He smoothed the paper flat so Brad could get a better look at it.

Leadership Roles and Behaviors

Leadership Roles and Behaviors	Provide	Counsel	Coach	Champion
Empathic Listening	△	▲	△	
Gathering Information	▲	△		
Clarifying Information	△	△	△	
Defining Expectations	▲	▲	△	
Sharing Intentions	△	▲	△	△
Exploring Options		△		△
Envisioning the Big Picture	△		▲	
Sponsoring Others				▲

"This has worked well for me, Brad. Does it make sense to you?"

Brad took the paper in his hand and studied it for a couple of minutes. He asked, "Are the dark symbols the primary behaviors and the lighter symbols the secondary ones?"

"Yes," said Mike. "This simple diagram has been invaluable to me, but I want to be sure it makes sense to you."

"I think so. Let me see if I have it right. First, I have to know which Role I will be using. How do I do that?"

"Good question. Through the years I've come up with two questions I always ask myself to determine which role will be most effective. They're simple and allow you to keep all the information I'm sharing into an easy to remember formula."

"Easy to remember is always a bonus," said Brad.

"First, I ask if the performance is above or below the line. If it's above the line, I am in the Coach or Champion role. If it's below the line, I know I am in either the Counsel or Provide role."

"That makes sense. And you're right, it's easy to remember," said Brad.

"The second question I ask is, Do I want the performance or behavior to change, stop, increase or continue? If the performance needs to Change, I use the Provide role. If the behavior or performance needs to Stop, I use the Counsel role. If I desire the performance to Increase or improve, I use the Coach role. I will use the Champion role when I want the performance to Continue on its course."

Mike paused and looked up at Brad who nodded. "It's really quite simple," Mike continued. "But don't be fooled by its simplicity. This is one of the most effective diagnostic tools you'll ever use in your capacity as a leader. And because it's so simple, it will quickly become second nature."

"That makes sense," said Brad. "I was just thinking about Empathic Listening and how it fits into diagnosing situations. What if I don't have all the information I need and I choose the wrong role?"

"You're really thinking this through. And, you're correct. What do you think needs to happen so you're absolutely sure which role you need to use?"

"I need to first listen with empathy so I can begin the process of sharing my intentions. That starts a two-way communication. Then I would engage in gathering information to understand exactly what is going on. You have to create a partnership where both parties are comfortable sharing their perspectives. I would gather as much information as I could and clarify that both of us have the same understanding. That way, the individual and I will both know which role is necessary. Once we are both sure of the correct role, I can look at the chart to tell me which behaviors I need to use to work through the issue."

"You know, Brad," Mike chuckled, "I've always said great minds think alike. You see it just like I do."

"Thanks, but hold onto that compliment. I may do some things differently than you would, but the core principles of the roles and behaviors are pretty sound."

"That's how I know you're getting it. You can think for yourself and incorporate these principles into your own talents and skill set. Every leader does things his or her own way. You can't be a cookie-cutter leader. You must be the leader you were meant to be."

"I'm glad I'm on the right track," said Brad.

Put it Together/Take Action

- Match Leadership Role and Behavior to the situation

- Leadership Roles: Provide, Counsel, Coach, Champion

- Behaviors: Empathic Listening, Gather Information, Clarify, Define Expectations, Share Intentions, Explore Options, Envision, Sponsor

26

Ready for Change

Before we go any further, let's evaluate where we are. I want to be sure we both see things the same way."

Brad responded, "Yeah, I think we are. So far, I'm okay with everything you've said. I'm starting to feel more comfortable with what you're teaching me. I think I'm ready to move on with the story. What happened the night you went home? Did you find a solution?"

"Yes, we did."

It took a lot of work on both our parts, but things turned out pretty well. After dinner I went outside on the back porch to think about my new friends and the predicament they were in. I had a problem I needed to solve and it didn't involve people, it involved frogs. How was I going to incorporate the very things I was learning from Bob and apply them to the situation at hand?

The problem with the pond would ultimately impact the actions I would take with my superiors. If I fought upper management, it was a sure bet I was going to lose. Yet, if I did nothing, the frogs would lose everything. There wasn't a thing I could control by working inside the company.

I sat for some time thinking over the fact that there was no way to influence what the company was doing. Then it struck me that this is how powerless many people feel when leaders and organizations make decisions that impact them. The impact is not only at work, but also in their personal lives as well. My experience had been that, generally, those in leadership don't seek much input from individuals. Often, business decisions are made with little regard to how they affect other people.

I thought again about Bob and the rest of the frogs. What options did I have? I didn't have any control at work, but I had control at home. So I thought about some options I could explore there. I mulled it over for a few minutes and then it came to me! I knew the solution!

I put some thoughts on paper, worked out a quick plan and went into the house to discuss the solution with my wife. She loved the idea. We had received a nice bonus the year before and the money was already there. I couldn't wait to tell Bob. Exploring Options really works!

Mike smiled broadly at Brad, as if everything had been explained.

"Come on!" Brad almost shouted. "Don't leave me in the dark. What was the solution?"

"Well, as it turns out, my house sits on over five acres of grass. I had to mow it every week and that took a huge chunk of time. Every time I mowed, I thought how nice it would be if I didn't have this much grass to deal with. My solution for Bob was also a solution for me—I'd put in a pond for Bob and the rest of the frogs. Two problems solved. Only half the grass to mow and I get to keep my friends."

"What did your wife think about you talking to a frog?" asked Brad.

"I didn't dare tell her at this point. She already thought I was a little crazy when we decided to buy such a large lot to build our house. Then I took the promotion, which meant a lot more work and much less time at home. She thought I was taking on way too much. Plus, she mentioned I'd been acting pretty strange the last few weeks. She didn't know I'd been spending that time talking to a frog."

I barely slept that night, I was so excited to tell Bob. I kept thinking about all the things I needed to do to make the plan work. The minute the sun hit my window I was up, showered, shaved and hurried to the pond before any other employees arrived. I figured I'd worry about breakfast later.

Bob arrived shortly after I sat down at the edge of the pond. He sat there in anticipation with a questioning look on his face. He could see I was tired and he was very concerned. "Any good news, Mike?" he asked.

"I have some good news and some bad news," I answered. "The bad news is the parking lot construction starts in about two weeks. There's nothing we can do about that. The good news is I think I have a solution. It will mean disrupting your entire lives and I'm sure not everyone will like it, but, I think it's worth a shot."

"You know I'm willing to explore all options, even when there's only one" said Bob. "Let's hear it."

"We're going to move all of you to a new pond!" I practically shouted. "I live about six miles from here on a huge plot of land. There are trees on three sides, with my house at the front. The point is, I have a great spot to build a pond! In fact, there's one spot already that dips somewhat, and it tends to fill with a little water when it rains a lot. It wouldn't take much to dig that out to make it into a real pond for you."

"You'd do that? For us?" Bob asked.

"Of course, I would!" I said. "We can provide a continuous source of fresh water. If I move quickly, I can have all of this done inside of ten days. It doesn't give us much room for error, so we'll have to get as many frogs on board as possible and come up with a plan to move the entire population from here to there. You may not have all the lily pads and other necessities at first, but with time you can build the pond the way you want."

Bob was speechless, so I just kept talking. "You know, some successful humans have a saying that applies here: *Just be steady, keep moving forward, and everything will work out.* Given the time constraints and other obstacles we're facing, I can't come up with any other options. What do you think?"

There was a long pause. Clearly Bob was weighing options. Finally, he said, "I know you haven't had much time and it looks like you've been up all night. But I still have to ask if there are any other options you've looked at and not shared?"

"A few," I responded. "But they're not very pleasant. However, you do have the right to know since it's your decision and your future. There are three other options. First, stay here, do nothing, and see what happens. I don't like that one, because bulldozers aren't very frog friendly. Second, I can take all of you to a pet store, where you may or may not find a home. The down side to this one is that I'm not sure what happens to frogs who aren't adopted. It might be as bad as the bulldozer. Last, the one I like the least, is I can take you to a restaurant where you would be the main course."

"Are you kidding?" Bob asked. "You don't have any better

options that those?"

I shrugged. What could I say? There just weren't a lot of social programs for homeless frogs.

Bob stared at me for a good while, then he broke out laughing. "Okay, okay. I had thought of those three options also, and like you said, none of them are acceptable. I also thought of relocating, but we're frogs, you know? It's not like we have maps of your world. Anything outside of the pond is a mystery to us."

Bob paused with a big sigh, then continued. "Out of the four options, the only one that makes sense is to relocate to your pond. But, please understand, this will mean we're putting our lives in your hands. We'll have to trust that you've embraced the Values of the Pond and that you will do what you say you will do. We have a lot of planning to do. After our session today I'll let all the frogs know your plan. We'll begin thinking about what it'll take to relocate and have a plan by tomorrow morning. Sound okay?"

"I guess it really does boil down to my character, and I understand the huge responsibility I'm taking on. I want to share my intentions with you. I do embrace the Values of the Pond and my intentions are to do what it takes to save you all."

"You have my complete trust, Mike," Bob said. "You've had it from the start and I'm sure the other frogs will trust you too. So, let's get working!"

Ready for Change

- *Focus only on what you can control*

- *Look outside the norm for solutions*

Moving the Pond

W ell, Brad, I know we're past our time," said Mike. "Can you spend a few more minutes with me and we'll complete the story?"

"I wouldn't let you go now for anything. Just let me call my wife so she won't worry about me."

"Would you like me to call her for you?" Mike asked with a laugh.

"No, she knows I've been meeting with you. I haven't told her about the frog part. In fact, I don't think I'll ever share that with her. I wish you had recorded Bob so you would have proof."

"Hold that thought. When I finish with the story you'll realize there's another person who also talked to Bob."

"Really! Who?"

"Just let me finish the story."

We had less than two weeks to get everything prepared to move Bob and the rest of the frogs. I was very busy getting a contractor to dig out the pond, put in a fresh water supply and prepare it for the frogs, and adding some fish and a little vegetation. He transplanted a few hundred lily pads from other ponds in the area and had the new pond filled and ready two days before construction on the parking lot began.

In the meantime, Bob and all the frogs were gathering vegetation, tadpoles, fish and anything else they needed to make a home in the new pond. He got quite a lot of resistance from many of the frogs. Most of the frogs still wouldn't believe that he was talking to a human. They could see us talking almost every day but didn't believe we were actually communicating.

I could see their point. This strange human warned him that heavy machinery was coming to destroy the pond and every creature's life was at risk. To make things worse, they would all have to get into containers to be moved to another pond. It was a huge risk for them.

Every frog in Bob's sector knew they could trust Bob so they began work immediately. Eventually, a good number of frogs from other sectors who knew of Bob's reputation began to trust him as well. Because they trusted Bob, they also trusted me. But some of the other lead frogs told their workers that the human had duped Bob. They were certain if they let themselves be put into containers, they would go right to pet stores or restaurants. No matter how hard Bob tried he couldn't convince everyone that change was coming their way.

I had suggested that we pause in our lessons because the frogs were working so hard all day. But Bob insisted we continue, and sometimes our discussions went late into the evenings. He wanted to make sure I learned and practiced as much as I could before the move.

With two days to spare, my wife and I drove our vehicles to the pond. I parked my truck as close to the pond as I could and pumped water into bins. Every square inch of the truck bed and most of the van was filled with containers. My wife, Anne, had a fish net with a long aluminum handle and caught as many fish as she could.

Then we turned our attention to the frogs. Imagine her surprise when many of the frogs hopped right into her net and let her put them into the containers! At first she thought it was a fluke, but when frog after frog jumped into her net, she said, "You'd think these frogs knew we were trying to help them!" I didn't enlighten her—I was still a little afraid to—and we collected as many of the frogs as would get into the net.

After a couple of hours, we had all of the frogs that had agreed to move, plus tadpoles and fish in the bins. My wife and I walked to the edge of the pond. Bob was sitting on his lily pad. He was the last frog to go. I looked at Bob and he looked at me. A silent communication took place and Bob nodded his head slightly in the affirmative. I didn't know what was going to happen so I just went for it. I turned to my wife, opened my mouth and said, pointing to Bob, "Dear, this is Bob. Bob, this is my wife Anne."

Anne looked at me, beyond bewildered. She gazed from me to Bob and back to me as if I were crazy. "Okay," she said. "What's going on here?"

Then it happened again. Bob came to my rescue and said to Anne, "Good evening, Anne. I've heard so much about you."

Anne just stood there, speechless, with her mouth wide open. She finally managed with great difficulty to speak one word, "W-w-w-w-what!"

Bob repeated, "Good evening, Anne. It's a pleasure to finally meet you. Are you okay?"

"No, I'm not okay!" she blurted. "I'm standing here, next to my husband, talking to a frog!" She turned to me and asked a little louder than I would have liked, "Is this why you've been acting so weird the past few weeks?"

I couldn't quit smiling. I was so happy that she was a part of this now. "Yes, dear," I said with total satisfaction. "I didn't think you'd believe me. This isn't the kind of thing you shout out to everyone. But, I'm so glad you're here, experiencing this with me."

"I need to sit down. Do you have an empty bin?"

"No, just sit on the ground, where I've been sitting almost every day the past few weeks. Welcome to my classroom."

"Mike, this isn't really happening, is it?" Anne asked, her voice shaking and doubt showing on her face. "Am I being filmed for some TV show?"

That one got me laughing uncontrollably. When I could talk again I said, "I'm afraid not. There aren't any cameras around. But to tell the truth, I'm so grateful this is happening. Now I know for sure I'm not crazy. Bob's been teaching me how to be an effective and productive leader. He's taught me the value of people in any organization. He's also taught me the value of frogs."

Bob then said, "Anne, can I have a few minutes with you and Mike before I get into a bin and you move us to our new pond?"

Anne was still questioning her sanity and simply said, "Sure, I would love nothing more than to sit here and listen to a frog. I mean you, Bob. I apologize for being rude but this is not what I expected when I came with Mike to help move some frogs to our pond."

"Don't think anything of it," said Bob. "Mike and I were even more surprised than you when we first spoke to each other. Now, before it gets too late I have a few things I'd like to share with Mike. Anne, feel free to ask any questions you'd like."

Having said that, Bob turned to me and with deep emotion began speaking. "Mike, my friend, you have been learning vital lessons. However, there is much more that I fear time will not allow us to cover. I don't know what will happen when we get to the new pond. You're probably going to have to figure out a lot more things on your own."

"I realize that, Bob," I said. "But I'm feeling fairly confident.

You've been a wonderful teacher."

"Just know that it will be a continual process," said Bob. "Don't be alarmed, that's part of learning how to lead your own way. Stay grounded and don't think you know more than everyone else. Be mindful of the power that will come as you learn to put your thoughts into action. Your leadership skills will be tested often. You will have successes and failures. Learn from both."

"Uncle Max always said you can learn more from failure than success," I said.

"That's true," said Bob. "The principles we've discussed together are a foundation to build upon, not a finished product. There's always something more that leaders can learn. Look for learning opportunities in every situation and problem you face. In fact, Mike, have you considered keeping all your notes from our times together?"

"Oh, you bet," I exclaimed. "I've been keeping quite a journal of all our discussions. After we meet, I go back to my office and expand on them with my thoughts and feelings. With some work it may even become a book to share with other future leaders. If that were to happen, with your permission I'd like to call it *Frogs Matter Most*.

Bob reflected on that and said, "That sounds like a great title to me. I'd be honored if you would use it."

Anne sat silently watching this exchange. It was clear from her face that she was not sure what to think or feel. However, a smile slowly replaced her stunned expression.

"I'm not entirely sure I understand all this," she said. "But I guess it's…possible? Or maybe being married to Mike has made me just as crazy as he is!" She laughed. I was relieved she was seeing the humor of the situation. "Mike, when you first got that new position, I was really worried about you. You were so stressed all the time. But now I'm thinking this explains why you've been coming home happier and more comfortable lately. Bob, I can see a new confidence in him that wasn't there before. She laughed again and said, "I know I'm seeing and hearing this, but it's still hard to believe."

"I don't blame your skepticism one bit," Bob said. "Have you noticed I waited to talk to you until the frogs who decided to come with us were safely in the truck? Many of them didn't believe me when I told them I was talking to Mike."

With a sense of sadness, Bob turned his head for a final look at the pond. "I worry what will happen to those who chose not to believe me."

"We did our best, Bob," I said in the most comforting tone I could muster. "Frogs and people have the right to choose for themselves. We'll take those who come with us and begin a new life in a new pond. We both know it will be much better for them to go through the pain of change rather than stay and do what they have always done and have it lead to their demise."

"I know, I know. It's still not a happy thought, losing some of my friends," Bob said with deep emotion.

"Bob," I said, looking over the pond. "Do you wish you could force them to come with us? It would be for their own good, after all."

"You would think that was a better option, wouldn't you? But always keep this in the forefront of your mind. Frogs, and people, have their agency. They have the right to choose. Watching others choose wrongly is one of the prices we pay for leadership. You learn to care about everyone and it hurts to see them make poor decisions."

All three of us sat looking at the pond, lost in our individual thoughts. It was getting dark and we could barely make out the far edges of the pond. Most of the frogs that chose to remain had gathered near Bob's lily pad. They glanced at us occasionally, but went about their business. They still didn't believe what was about to happen in just two day's time.

"Now wait just a minute!" Brad interrupted. "Why didn't you just gather them all up, whether they wanted to go or not? Don't you think they would've eventually thanked you for saving them, even if it was against their will."

"Possibly, but frogs do things much the same way humans do," said Mike. "Bob explained to me that, in their culture, you honored each frog's right to choose. As painful as it was for Bob and for me, we let them stay."

"But you didn't give up, did you?"

"What could we do?" asked Mike. "I left a couple of containers by the pond, so they had a way out if they changed their minds. A few jumped in over the next two days, but not many. We still had hope that those who remained would see the machinery moving in and hurry to a new location in time. Hopefully, they made it out to a safe place."

Mike shook his head and sighed. "I don't know what happened. I didn't go to work during the few days they filled in the pond and covered it with blacktop. It was just too difficult. I told myself it was because we needed a few days to help the frogs get settled. But, honestly, I was afraid to see what would happen to the frogs that chose to remain. That was the last time I saw the pond."

Brad was silent, so Mike continued.

I knelt down, held out my hand and Bob hopped onto my palm. We walked quietly to the truck where I gently let Bob down into a bin. He looked up at me and said, "Mike, thanks for all you're doing for us. Without even knowing it, you've demonstrated the

Values of the Pond— Respect, Integrity and Loyalty—throughout our short relationship and our many conversations. Even though we know humans don't consider frogs to be equals, you showed me and all the other frogs respect. You listened. You learned. You cared. That takes great humility and respect."

"Thank you," I said. I was really touched.

"You've done everything you said you would do," said Bob. "That's integrity. And, you've done everything because it was the right thing to do, not because it would benefit you personally. It has been said, and I agree, that *character is how you treat those who can do nothing for you.* We know you can't possibly benefit from saving us. Lastly, you've shown tremendous loyalty to us by being willing to sacrifice a portion of your property to preserve our entire community and way of life."

I looked at Bob, stunned that he was so generous with his praise. I finally responded. "Bob, I can't tell you what our relationship means to me. You have embodied the very things you've taught me. You've motivated me to do the same for other future leaders, when it's their time to lead and my turn to teach. I now know leadership is a difficult yet worthwhile endeavor. It requires temperance in a way I've never thought about before. By temperance, I mean a balance between getting the job done and valuing people. You've shown me you don't have to sacrifice one to accomplish the other. In fact, when you put frogs, or people first, amazing things can happen."

We looked at each other for a long couple of minutes, silently sharing our friendship. There was appreciation and respect in both our faces. We knew a special bond had been shared.

Bob interrupted the special moment of silence. "So, I guess we'll pick up our discussions after we are settled in the new pond?"

"I can't wait to learn about the process of how to maintain what you've taught me through a long-term relationship with my people," I said.

"I don't know if I've figured all that out yet," admitted Bob. "But together. maybe we can create a sequel to your *Frogs Matter Most* book."

"Great! I look forward to that," I said.

I jumped up and got into the truck. Anne got into her van. We began the trip home.

Moving the Pond

- *Work along side your people*

- *Don't be afraid to get your hands dirty*

- *Frogs and people matter most*

28

A New Start

How did Bob and his frogs like the new pond?" Brad asked. "Did they adjust? Are they okay? How did everything turn out?"

Mike laughed and said, "You're getting ahead of me. Like I said, I didn't see the demolition of the pond. All I know is the following week the construction crews came in, rerouted the spring that fed the pond, drained the remaining water, and filled the pond with dirt. After the dirt settled, they paved the parking lot as you see it today. I didn't see what happened to the other frogs. But Bob and his frogs were another story."

Bob and his friends seemed to love the new pond. They had a fresh start to build whatever they wanted. They were very busy the next two weeks. I didn't see Bob during that time because they were so occupied. I had a lot of catching up at work to do, too.

I looked forward to going out and meeting with Bob to resume our conversations. After the first couple of weeks I went

to the pond a few times, but Bob didn't show up at all. He must
have been busier than I thought.

Finally, at the end of the fourth week, I walked to the pond
with Anne to see if we could find Bob. There he was, waiting for us
on a new lily pad. The pond looked beautiful! They had put their
mark on it. We waved to him and he waved back.

When we were only a few feet away from the edge of the pond,
I said, "Hey, Bob. How are you?"

We waited for an answer, but instead of talking he croaked a
reply. I figured that was his new way of saying hello. I knelt down
at the edge and asked, "Bob, how are things going with the new
pond?"

Again, all Anne and I heard was a soft croak. He continued
sitting on the lily pad with what looked like a smile on his face, he
waved and croaked again.

I guess he could see the confused expression on my face
because he croaked once more. Then again. It was finally obvious,
even to him, that there was a problem. He shrugged his shoulders
and held his two, three-fingered hands up in frustration.

It was over. Bob and I never talked again.

For a couple of months after, when I'd walk down to the pond,
Bob would come sit on his lily pad and wave. I would sit on the
edge of the pond and talk as though he could still understand me.
He would croak every now and then. Anne would often join me
and I would share the things Bob had taught me.

The last time I saw him was a warm day in late autumn. Now
that I look back on that day, Bob sat on the lily pad and watched
me a little longer than usual. It was as if he knew we wouldn't see
each other again. He gave me a blink, and then he was gone.

A New Start

- Not everyone will choose to follow

- Never impose your will on others

- Allow for individual agency

29

Teaching Forward

M ike stopped talking. Brad sat in his chair, looking out the window at the parking lot. Neither spoke for a while.

Brad finally looked at Mike and said, "I know it's crazy, but I believe it. I believe all of it. I know you as a leader and I know you're a man of character and loyalty. I believe every word you have spoken."

Mike laughed and responded, "Thanks. Do you believe me enough to continue our discussions?"

"I've already been writing things down," Brad said. "Didn't you say you wrote what Bob taught you?"

"Yes I did and I have that information, but there's so much more," Mike said. "I learned from Bob how to approach leadership with respect, integrity and loyalty. First I had to care enough to lead in a way people would be willing to follow."

Brad nodded. These concepts were becoming more and more familiar. He almost could guess what was coming next.

"My next challenge was learning to diagnose every situation to determine which role was needed," said Mike. "It wasn't as hard as I thought it would be. If the performance was above the line,

I knew I would be in either the Coach or the Champion role. If the performance was below the line, I would act in the Counsel or Provide roles. After that, it was a matter of engaging in the primary behaviors of each role. I saw great success right away."

"And you continue to see success," said Brad. "I've watched you closely, especially since we've started these discussions."

"Thank you, Brad. I was hoping you had observed and appreciated my leadership style. However, as Bob taught, leadership is a continuous process. Although he and I didn't have the chance to go any further, I'd like us to continue exploring these concepts. Would you be willing to do that?"

"I certainly would," said Brad.

"Good," said Mike. "I'd like you to write down the lessons you learn in our continuing discussions. Bob and I had talked about the process to implement his lessons into long-term actionable events and discussions with people using the behaviors, roles and values. You and I will have future discussions on how to implement this in an ongoing relationship with everyone you lead."

"Mike, I can hardly wait. And I'll bring a recorder to every session. I don't want to miss a word."

"Thanks for spending so much time with me after work hours," said Mike. "I think we're done here today. Let's go home. Tomorrow, we'll figure out a schedule for our discussions on the leadership processes."

"Okay, I'll see you in the morning. Thanks, Mike."

Mike walked to his car and sat for a few minutes, looking across the parking lot, remembering his many visits at the pond's edge with Bob. He drove home and found Anne in the kitchen preparing dinner.

He gave her a hug and asked, "How about we take a stroll out to the pond?"

She took his hand with a smile and they walked together out to the pond. They gazed over the water and talked about how much beauty it had added to their property. They sat down in the gazebo they had built on the pond's edge. Mike looked at Anne and said, "Thank you for believing me."

"Well, I wouldn't have if I hadn't heard Bob with my own ears," Anne said. "I'm so proud of the leader, husband, and man you have become. It's been a true joy watching you grow. Now, don't you think it's time you took Bob's place and shared these things with other leaders who are willing to listen?"

"You know you have a great idea. I have a lot written down and Bob liked the title I gave it. Do you think people would read a book with the title, *Frogs Matter Most*?"

"Well, they sure won't if you don't write it," Anne said as she pulled him close, put her arms around his neck and kissed his lips gently.

Teaching Forward

- *Learn from your mistakes*

- *Teach, teach, teach*

30

Believing

*B*rad waited a few minutes before leaving the office. He walked to his car, thinking on Mike's incredible story about learning leadership from a frog. It still sounded unbelievable to him. He looked over the parking lot and thought about what it would have been like talking with Bob. He shook his head. He'd have to think about it later. He needed to get home.

As he drove home, thoughts of Bob and Mike continued to run through Brad's mind. He parked his car in the garage, then walked around to the front door to pick up the newspaper. He folded it in half and put it under his arm as he entered the house.

"Hi everybody, I'm home," he called.

No one answered so he went into the kitchen and saw a note on the counter. His wife and daughter had gone to the grocery store to pick up a few items. They would be back shortly.

He took the paper to his favorite chair in the living room and began reading, but he couldn't concentrate. In his mind, he kept going back to the pond and Mike's conversations with Bob. Did it really happen? Or was Mike just using it as a teaching method to help him be a better leader? *Talking frogs—come on!* He thought as he turned the page of his newspaper.

Just then his wife and daughter opened the door leading from the garage. His daughter came through the kitchen and ran to him. "Daddy!" she cried. "I've been waiting all day for you to come home. I forgot to tell you about what I learned at church the other day. There was a man who had a donkey, and the donkey talked to him! Can you believe that?"

Brad looked at his daughter with a smile. As he put his hand on her cheek he thought about Bob, the talking Disney characters, and the talking animals in C.S. Lewis books. "Yes, sweetheart, I think I can believe it. Come sit on my lap and tell me more."

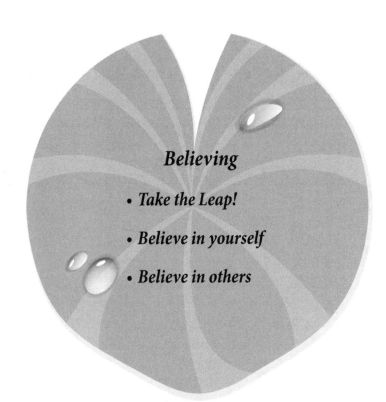

Believing

- *Take the Leap!*
- *Believe in yourself*
- *Believe in others*

About the Authors

Dr. Jack R. Christianson has been a leader in large organizations in the public and private sector. He holds a Doctor of Philosophy Degree in Educational Sociology from the University of Buckingham in England.

Jack has lectured and given seminars all across the United States and Canada to all ages and types of organizations. He is the author of numerous inspirational books and many audio recordings.

He and his wife Melanie Harris are the parents of four daughters and one son.

www.jackrchristianson.com

Ron M. Tracy is the founder of Tracy Learning and has over 25 years of corporate training and consulting experience. He is recognized as a master trainer in leadership, team development, critical thinking skills, customer service, and peer mentoring.

Ron has authored several highly successful training programs and worked with many Fortune 500 companies to develop and implement training strategies.

He and his wife, Deniece are the parents of four daughters, one son and grandparents of eighteen grandchildren.

www.tracylearning.com

If you are interested in making *Frogs Matter Most* part of your corporate culture, please visit our website for information about speaking engagements or our two-day workshop.

www.frogsmattermost.com